THE MANAGER'S GUIDE TO MAXIMIZING EMPLOYEE POTENTIAL

THE MANAGER'S GUIDE TO MAXIMIZING EMPLOYEE POTENTIAL

Quick and Easy
Strategies to Develop Talent
Every Day

William J. Rothwell

American Management Association
New York • Atlanta • Brussels • Chicago • Mexico City
San Francisco • Shanghai • Tokyo • Toronto • Washington, D. C

Special discounts on bulk quantities of AMACOM books are available to corporations, professional associations, and other organizations. For details, contact Special Sales Department, AMACOM, a division of American Management Association, 1601 Broadway, New York, NY 10019. Tel: 800-250-5308. Fax: 518-891-2372.
E-mail: specialsls@amanet.org
Website: www.amacombooks.org/go/specialsales
To view all AMACOM titles go to: www.amacombooks.org

This publication is designed to provide accurate and authoritative information in regard to the subject matter covered. It is sold with the understanding that the publisher is not engaged in rendering legal, accounting, or other professional service. If legal advice or other expert assistance is required, the services of a competent professional person should be sought.

Library of Congress Cataloging-in-Publication Data

Rothwell, William J., 1951–
The manager's guide to maximizing employee potential : quick and easy strategies to develop talent every day / by William J. Rothwell.
    p.   cm.
Includes index.
ISBN 978-0-8144-1430-9
1. Manpower planning. 2. Career development. 3. Employees—Training of. 4. Performance technology. I. Title.
HF5549.5.M3R662   2010
658.3′124—dc22

                                                                            2009014407

Printing number

10 9 8 7 6 5 4 3 2 1

Contents

Preface

What do you, as a manager, have to do with recruiting, developing, and retaining talent? The short answer is simple: *you have everything to do with those activities.* It is not the human resource (HR) department's job to manage talent. Although HR professionals do have parts to play in talent management—and so do CEOs, top managers, and even individuals—it is not the HR department's job to build talent *on a daily basis.* One reason is simply that managers see workers all the time, while HR professionals interact with them on fewer occasions. Because most talent development occurs on the job and not in training classrooms off the job, it just makes sense to conclude that each worker's supervisor bears a major responsibility for talent management. Therefore, this book focuses on the tactical, rather than the strategic, issues involved in how talent is managed and developed.

Of course, many managers claim they are simply too busy getting the work out to recruit, develop, and retain talent. But managing talent is what they should be doing routinely; it should not be considered an additional or onerous task. It is the essence of what management is all about. To do this properly, managers must simultaneously complete the day's work while still preparing employees for the future. Doing that requires skillful juggling.

This book consists of 14 chapters about the manager's role in developing talent. Chapter 1 is entitled "The Importance of Talent Management." It defines talent management and related terms, explains why managers should focus attention on the subject, how they should accomplish their goals in this area, why talent management deserves attention, and how to manage worker expectations. Chapter 2 focuses on grooming a replacement, while Chapter 3 goes right to the heart of talent management by describing how managers can recognize the potential for greatness in people who have not yet shown it. Chapter 4 continues the discussion by describing practical recruiting and selection techniques that can support talent management for your department and the organization of which you are part. Then, Chapter 5 challenges the sometimes prevailing notion that "sending people out" is the best way to develop them. It describes how managers can plan workers' job assignments so as to build their competencies while also getting work out of them. Chapter 6 focuses on career planning and career counseling; Chapter 7 on performance and development coaching; and Chapter 8 on the manager's role in appraising workers and providing real-time feedback.

The next group of chapters—Chapters 9, 10, and 11—deal with managing high potential and high professional workers, transferring knowledge and professional contacts, and working with diverse people. The final three chapters—Chapters 12, 13, and 14—describe how managers should work with diverse people, manage problem performers and decruitment, and set an example for workers through self-development. The two appendixes answer some frequently-asked questions about talent management and offer the start of a daily calendar for planning your efforts to manage and develop talent.

Throughout this book, you will find practical tips. Each is presented as a sidebar and deserves special attention.

Acknowledgments

To be effective as talent developers, managers must be more than merely *managers*—they must be *leaders*. Leadership is a term that is bandied about much these days. But, in simple terms, a leader is anyone who influences other people. And managers, as leaders, must influence others to realize their full potential.

Many people have influenced me. Some by being supportive; some by being "difficult"; and, some by simply "being there" when I needed someone to talk to, commiserate with, or get advice from. To all these people, I would like to express my sincerest thanks.

Thanks to my wife, Marcelina, and to my daughter, Candice, for just being there for me. They are the wind beneath my wings.

Thank you to my training session participants, both in the United States and many other nations, who have shaped my thinking on this topic. A special thanks to my friend Peter Chee at ITD in Malaysia and to managers at Bank Mandiri in Indonesia, where I first presented the topic of this book to all the key managers. I also wish to thank people who reviewed this book in early drafts and offered advice. They include Jim Graber of Business Decisions Inc. and Bob Prescott, Professor of HR at Rollins College in Orlando, Florida.

Thanks to my graduate assistant, Lin Gao, who helped secure the necessary permissions for this book. And thanks to the managers and the high potentials to whom I have spoken during the preparation and research of this book for their encouragement and their ideas. While you are anonymous in the book, you know who you are.

A special thank you to Christina Parisi, my editor at AMACOM, for her support in helping this book reach the press.

Advance Organizer

What Do You as a Manager Do on a Daily Basis to Support Talent Management?

Directions:

Use this advance organizer to reflect on how well you and other managers in your organization develop talented people on a *daily* basis. For each action listed in the left column, rate *all* managers (not just yourself) in your organization in the center column. (If you score the item poorly, then find in the right column the chapter in this book where the topic is treated.) Score your results at the end of the organizer. Use the following scale for the ratings in the center column:

5 = Performed very well by managers in this organization
4 = Performed well by managers in this organization
3 = Performed somewhat well by managers in this organization
2 = Performed poorly by managers in this organization
1 = Performed very poorly by managers in this organization
0 = Not applicable to this organization

Exhibit 1. The Advance Organizer

How Well Do Managers Carry This Out in Your Organization?	Rate the Quality of How Well Managers Do This in Your Organization						Chapter in This Book Where the Topic Is Treated
Managers in this organization generally...	0	1	2	3	4	5	
1 Recognize the need to develop talent	0	1	2	3	4	5	1
2 Are willing to develop talent on a daily basis	0	1	2	3	4	5	1
3 Know how to get work out of people effectively on a daily basis	0	1	2	3	4	5	1
4 Are aware of the strategic objectives for talent development in the organization	0	1	2	3	4	5	1
5 Take active steps to identify and develop their backups in case of emergency	0	1	2	3	4	5	2
6 Assess individual potential on a daily basis	0	1	2	3	4	5	3
7 Recruit talented people on a daily basis	0	1	2	3	4	5	4
8 Select or participate in selecting talented people on a daily basis	0	1	2	3	4	5	4
9 Train talented people on a daily basis	0	1	2	3	4	5	5
10 Develop talented people on a daily basis	0	1	2	3	4	5	5
11 Encourage individuals to plan for their careers	0	1	2	3	4	5	6
12 Offer career counseling	0	1	2	3	4	5	6
13 Effectively offer performance coaching	0	1	2	3	4	5	7
14 Effectively offer development coaching	0	1	2	3	4	5	7
15 Appraise workers	0	1	2	3	4	5	8
16 Provide daily feedback about performance	0	1	2	3	4	5	8
17 Manage high-potental workers effectively	0	1	2	3	4	5	9
18 Manage high-professional workers effectively	0	1	2	3	4	5	9
19 Encourage knowledge transfer	0	1	2	3	4	5	10
20 Encourage the transfer of professional contacts	0	1	2	3	4	5	10

How Well Do Managers Carry This Out in Your Organization?		Rate the Quality of How Well Managers Do This in Your Organization						Chapter in This Book Where the Topic Is Treated
Managers in this organization generally...		0	1	2	3	4	5	
21	Retain talented people	0	1	2	3	4	5	11
22	Work with diverse people effectively	0	1	2	3	4	5	12
23	Decruit people who are not well suited for their jobs	0	1	2	3	4	5	13
24	Model development by developing themselves	0	1	2	3	4	5	14
25	Demonstrate special competencies to build talent on a daily basis	0	1	2	3	4	5	2

Add up your scores and place the number here   ▶   _____

Scoring

If your score is	Then
125–101	Congratulations! Your organization is unusual—in a good way. Give your organization an "A."
100–76	Managers in your organization are doing a pretty good job—but could still stand to improve. Read selected chapters of this book and brainstorm on ways to apply the lessons contained in this book. Managers in your organization deserve a "B."
75–51	Give managers in your organization a "C." More attention must be paid by managers to talent management on a daily basis.
50–26	Give managers in your organization a "D." Attention must be paid *now* by managers to talent management on a daily basis.
25–0	Give managers in your organization an "F" for talent management. Attention must be paid *now* by managers to applying talent management on a daily basis.

THE MANAGER'S GUIDE TO MAXIMIZING EMPLOYEE POTENTIAL

1

The Importance of Talent Management

Every day you are juggling. In fact, juggling could be a metaphor for modern business. Another way to describe this is *multi-tasking*. You know what that means—doing more than one thing at a time. It means, for instance, talking on the phone while also writing an e-mail. Today, successful managers are master jugglers who know how to multitask to increase their daily output to two or three times that of the average person. If you are really good at it, juggling is so interwoven into what you do that you hardly even think about it.

Juggling is a good metaphor for the activities required to manage and develop talent. On the one hand, your workers must meet each day's work requirements. At the same time, you should be developing their talents for future and, perhaps, higher level responsibilities.

Many questions need to be considered. How do you meet current work expectations while developing talent? What is talent management, and what other terms are related to it (and are sometimes confused with it)? How do you manage talent? Why is your daily involvement critically important? How do you manage expectations? This chapter answers these questions.

DEFINING TALENT MANAGEMENT AND OTHER RELEVANT TERMS

Talent management is a term in search of a meaning. It can mean many different things and has no "standard definition." Taken together, the words *talent management* can mean the act of handling, directing and controlling *star performers*—that is, those in the organization who possess a special natural ability or aptitude. In daily conversation, most managers understand that *talent management means integrated efforts to recruit, develop, and keep the best and most talented people.*

One could debate whether managers should focus their efforts on just the top 1 to 10 percent of the most productive and promotable people in an organization or whether everyone has talent that managers and individuals need to discover and develop. Generally, however, most talent management authorities focus on talent management as an investment strategy designed to make the most of the best—that is, they focus on those who are both most productive and most promotable. (You may wish to think about your own philosophy and that of your own organization in this regard.) One justification for this approach is that high-potential performers can be up to twenty times more productive than average performers. As a result, investments in their development can yield higher rewards for the organization.

Talent management should not be confused with related terms, such as:

- *Replacement planning:* The process of identifying short-term or long-term back ups in case of emergency.

- *Succession planning:* The process of identifying individuals to be developed inside an organization.
- *Succession management:* The daily process of preparing people for more responsibility.
- *Work force planning:* The process of reexamining all the people in an organization to determine if their collective talents are sufficient to achieve the organization's strategic objectives.

HOW TO MANAGE TALENT

As a manager or supervisor, you should take the following daily steps to manage the talented people reporting to you.

- Identify short-term and long-term back ups for your own work.
- Assess individual potential.
- Recruit and select talented people.
- Train and develop talented people.
- Encourage career planning and offer career counseling.
- Carry out performance and development coaching.
- Appraise workers and provide daily feedback.
- Manage high-potential and high-professional workers.
- Transfer knowledge and professional contacts.
- Retain talent.
- Work with diverse people.
- Decruit people who are not performing properly after exhausting other efforts.
- Set an example by modeling self-development.

Consider the model appearing in Exhibit 1-1.

You should be taking the list above to heart. It is what you should be doing *every day.* If you push back and say, "Well, I would like to do that, but I just don't have time for it," then I would say

Exhibit 1-1. What Managers Should Do Every Day to Manage Talent

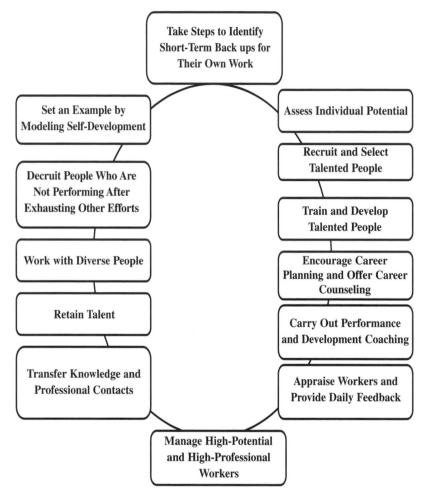

you were giving a lame excuse. Learn how to work smarter, not harder. Learn how to attract, develop, manage and retain talent while also getting the work you need out of people every day.

A fact of modern management life is that, as a result of down-sizing and other staffing changes, many managers devote only about

10 percent of their time to dealing with people and perhaps as much as 90 percent analyzing data or doing work themselves. But you still need to plan for, and act on, the need for business continuity. This cannot be accomplished at the strategic level only. It must also happen with you, every day, at the tactical level.

WHY THE MANAGER'S DAILY INVOLVEMENT IS CRITICALLY IMPORTANT IN TALENT MANAGEMENT

What you do every day is critically important to talent management. In addition to the list of items on page 3, consider that you are the one who:

- Serves as a role model to your people about how a manager should behave.
- Encourages—or discourages—employee behavior by how you act, what you say, and what you pay attention to or choose to ignore. (That means managers obsessed with details will tend to make their employees that way; managers who are very imaginative will build the same competencies in those who work for them).
- Provides advice about how your employees should prepare for the future—and, remember, they don't know what to do because they have never done what you do.

Think for a moment about how well you do each of these activities on a daily basis. Use the worksheet appearing in Exhibit 1-2 to assess yourself and ponder ways to improve how well you carry out these activities linked to talent management on a daily basis.

Exhibit 1-2. A Worksheet on Assessing and Improving Your Role as a Daily Manager of Talent

Directions: Use this worksheet to reflect on your daily role as a manager of talent. For each item listed in the left column below, comment on your ability in the center column and indicate how you think you could improve in the right column.

What a Manager Should Do on a Daily Basis to Manage Talent		How Well Do You Feel You Perform the Role as a Manager of Talent on a Daily Basis?	What Do You Think You Could Do to Improve Yourself as a Manager of Talent on a Daily Basis?
1	Serve as a role model to your people about how a manager should behave		
2	Encourage—or discourage—employee behavior by how you act, what you say, and what you pay attention to or choose to ignore. (That means a manager obsessed with details will tend to make his or her employees that way; a manager who is very imaginative will build the same competencies in those who work for him or her)		
3	Provide advice about how your employees should prepare for the future—and, remember, they don't know what to do because they have never done what you do		
4	Take steps to identify short-term and long-term back ups for their own work		

What a Manager Should Do on a Daily Basis to Manage Talent		How Well Do You Feel You Perform the Role as a Manager of Talent on a Daily Basis?	What Do You Think You Could Do to Improve Yourself as a Manager of Talent on a Daily Basis?
5	Assess individual potential		
6	Recruit and select talented people		
7	Train and develop talented people		
8	Encourage career planning and offer career counseling		
9	Appraise workers and provide daily feedback		
10	Manage high-potential and high-professional workers		
11	Transfer knowledge and professional contacts		
12	Retain talent		
13	Work with diverse people		
14	Decruit people who are not performing properly after exhausting other efforts		
15	Set an example of self-development		
16	What other activities should a manager perform on a daily basis to be effective as a manager of talent? (List)		

THE MANAGER'S DAILY RESPONSIBILITIES IN MANAGING PERSONAL EXPECTATIONS

You influence your workers in ways that you have never realized. How you treat people—not just what you say but your body language also—shows how you regard them. That can affect the results you get from them.

Have you ever heard of the idea of a self-fulfilling prophecy? *It is the belief that an otherwise unproven or even erroneous notion can be proven true just because someone believes it to be true.* The self-fulfilling prophecy is seen nearly every day on Wall Street. If investors lose confidence in a company's management or in the economy, the stock price of one company or all companies will plummet. Some would say that is exactly what happened to Enron. Investors lost confidence in company managers, and Enron went bankrupt almost overnight, even though it had many assets.

The same principle applies to your expectations of your workers. In the management literature, it is sometimes called the *Pygmalion effect.* It is related to something else called the *Galatea effect.* What do these principles mean? How do they relate to talent management? What guidance can they provide in managing talent every day?

The Pygmalion Effect

In the classic poem *Metamorphoses,* the Roman poet Ovid told the story of Pygmalion. Pygmalion was king of Cyprus. He sculpted an image of an outstandingly beautiful woman named Galatea. The statue was so beautiful that the king fell in love with his creation. The classic gods of Ancient Rome took pity on Pygmalion and brought the statue to life.

The Pygmalion effect has important implications for managers. *It is a specific kind of self-fulfilling prophecy that indicates that when a manager has a high or low opinion of an individual or a group, that individual or group will live up to (or down to) those expectations.* Managers reveal their expectations both consciously (through what they say and do) and unconsciously (through their body language).

Other names for this are the *Rosenthal effect* or *teacher expectancy effect*. First described in a 1978 research article by R. Rosenthal and D. B. Rubin in the journal, *Behavioural and Brain Sciences,* it takes its name from researcher Robert Rosenthal, who has examined how peoples' beliefs can influence their perceptions of reality. A famous experiment conducted by Jane Elliott, an internationally renowned teacher and recipient of the prestigious National Mental Health Association Award for Excellence in Education, illustrated the power of the teacher expectancy effect. A group of blue-eyed children were selected at random to participate in a now-famous experiment. Then, she introduced the children to a group of teachers who were told that these children were selected because they had extremely high intelligence. During the year in which the children studied with these teachers, they were consistently rated as high performers. The implication is that it was the teachers' high expectations of the children, and not the performance of the children themselves, that led to the high rating.

The same principles can apply to you as a manager. If you believe your workers are exceptionally talented, the chances are they will live up to those expectations. But if you believe they are exceptionally stupid or lazy, they will live down to those expectations. Consequently, a critically important issue in talent management is your perceptions of your workers.

The Galatea Effect

An important corollary of the Pygmalion effect is the *Galatea effect.* Galatea was the name of the beautiful woman whose statue was carved by Pygmalion. Simply stated, the Galatea effect means that your workers come to believe in their own exceptional talents as a direct result of how you treat them. Your expectations, as communicated through your unconscious behaviors, create a self-fulfilling prophecy that can make them exceptionally talented. In short, your behavior as a manager affects how much people believe in themselves. When you show immense faith in their talents and build up their self-esteem and self-confidence, they live up to your expectations because they believe in themselves. The Galatea effect means that workers come to internalize the unconditional positive regard you feel for them and show them.

What Do These Principles Mean?

The importance of the Pygmalion effect and the Galatea effect on talent management cannot be overstated. You get what you expect. Perception shapes reality. Your expectations of others influence reality and can even affect how the workers perceive themselves and behave in line with their own expectations

Start by reflecting on how you feel and what you believe about all workers—and then about your own workers in particular. How do *you* think you treat them? How would *they say* you treat them?

As you begin that self-reflection, review Douglas McGregor's Theory X and Y, which is also based on management's perceptions of people. To McGregor, Theory X managers generally believe that employees are inherently lazy and will do everything possible to avoid work. Consequently, they must be closely watched, controlled, and supervised. Employees will do only what they are paid to do. Theory X managers often blame others when things go wrong and think people are selfishly motivated.

In contrast, Theory Y managers take a more positive view of human nature. According to McGregor, Y managers assume that each individual is capable of assuming more responsibility. People can be self-motivated and self-directed. Theory Y managers believe that many people find meaning in the work they do and generally want to do a good job. Such managers feel that their job is to identify and knock down the organizational barriers that prevent workers from reaching their peak performance and potential. By doing that, Theory Y managers create a work environment that leads to higher degrees of worker engagement and commitment.

What kind of manager are you? A Theory X or a Theory Y manager?

Remember that workers can become demotivated and disengaged based on bureaucratic rules and red tape, tight controls, and management behavior that is not supportive. Even highly talented people will grow discouraged when they feel that their efforts are not rewarded or appreciated.

Now consider, what do *you* believe about:

- The nature of people in general? (Are people basically good, bad, or somewhere in between?)
- Your workers in particular?
- The nature of work? (Is work good, bad, or somewhere in between?)
- The quality of work performed by your workers?
- The talent level of your workers?
- The unique strengths and talents of each of your workers?
- The areas in which all of your workers could stand to improve?
- How *your* behavior affects your workers?
- How you could demonstrate a more positive regard for all your workers?
- What motivates people?

The lesson to be learned here is that, to paraphrase total quality guru W. Edwards Deming, management creates most of its own problems by the way it sets up the work environment. Management behavior is an important part of that environment. How managers act—and that means *you*—can and does affect the talent of the organization. Talented people will not flourish in an environment that does not encourage them, and they will not grow when their managers take them for granted, don't challenge them, or have a low regard for them.

How Do These Principles Relate to What You Should Do in Setting Expectations Every Day?

How you feel about your workers affects how they perform. Never forget that. It means that if you want to mount an improvement effort, you must begin with yourself—and how you behave. Consider:

What you say

- Do you tell people that you believe they are talented?
- Do you express support for people?
- Do you encourage people when they express uncertainty in their ability to perform?

What you do

- Do you take pains to show that you appreciate the efforts that people make?
- Do you show your people, through your daily actions, that you believe they are talented?

What your nonverbal and body language says

- Does your body language support what you say and do?
- Do you look at people in ways that show that you care about them?
- Do you pay attention to people, or do you allow yourself to be distracted by the phone, e-mails, or interruptions?
- Do you look at your watch or look away when people are asking you a question?
- Do you lean toward people when you listen to them?

APPLICATION QUESTIONS

1. How would you define *talent?* How much do you believe it exists in each worker and is up to the individual and his or her supervisor to identify and cultivate, and how much do you believe that organizations should focus on attracting, developing, and retaining workers who are both productive in their present jobs and also promotable to higher level responsibility?

2. Talk to other managers in your organization. Ask them what *they do* to attract, develop, and retain workers. Listen carefully to what they say.

3. Pick several of your own best workers. Ask them: (1) What should the organization be doing to encourage them to bring recommendations for especially productive and promotable people to recruit? (2) What should the organization be doing to develop them on the job every day? (3) What should the organization be doing to build a climate in which people want to stay?

4. Reflect on the Pygmalion and the Galatea effects. How much do you see evidence of these in your own organization? What specific behaviors could you demonstrate on a daily basis to build people's self-esteem while also developing them?

2

Identifying and Grooming a Replacement

While talent management is not the same as replacement planning, it just makes sense to start with the most basic need of most organizations—that is, continuity planning in case of the sudden short-term or long-term loss of a key person (like yourself!). Your first responsibility as a manager is to identify and train someone to back you up in case you are out because of vacation, illness, death, disability, or a sudden wonderful event (like winning the lottery to the tune of a cool $100 million after taxes.).

So, what is replacement planning? Why is it important? How can you identify back ups for the short term and long term? Should you tell people that they are on a replacement chart? How can you act on the information that you obtain from replacement charting? How can you groom a replacement once identified? What mistakes should you avoid in identifying and grooming a replacement? This chapter answers these questions.

REPLACEMENT PLANNING DEFINED

Replacement planning is the simplest form of continuity planning for people. It assumes that the organization's leaders will retain the existing organizational structure (organization chart) and will find individuals to fill key positions. Replacement planning seeks back ups for all important positions on the organization chart. *Short-term replacement planning* focuses on back ups who are good enough to do your work while you are gone for a short time due to sickness or vacation. *Long-term replacement planning* is a form of risk management that identifies individuals who can fill in for you over an extended period in case of death, disability, or an unexpected resignation. While it may be desirable to have several people fully prepared to do your work, a more typical goal is to have up to three qualified replacements identified in advance who can at least serve in an "acting" capacity (a holding action) long enough for the organization to do a proper search to fill the vacancy with a fully qualified person. Of course, that person may be the back up.

THE IMPORTANCE OF REPLACEMENT PLANNING

How will your organization survive if one or more key people are suddenly lost due to a tragic accident or a wonderful event like winning the lottery? Replacement planning for people is just as important—and perhaps even more so—than planning for the unexpected loss of money, facilities, equipment, or data. Yet many managers do not think to do it, perhaps because it reminds them of their own deaths—or they are worried that their organizations will replace them with those who are younger or not so well paid!

Still, both short-term and long-term planning is essential to ensure business continuity. "The show must go on" whether you are at work or are suddenly taken ill.

IDENTIFYING BACK UPS FOR THE SHORT TERM AND LONG TERM

Start with a picture of your department as it appears on a typical organization chart (See Exhibit 2–1.) Identify all your key reports. Then, for yourself and all your key reports, identify people from inside the organization who could reasonably be considered back ups. Complete the chart. Rank "1," your top back up, is the person best prepared to fill in on a short-term or long-term basis. If you cannot identify three possible back ups for each position, then identify the ones for which you *can* identify back ups. If you cannot identify any back ups, note that on the chart. You may wish to create different charts for short-term and long-term back ups if there is need.

Then, for each position, indicate whether the people you identified are able to do the job right now without any further need for development. If so, code the "readiness" as RN (meaning *ready now*). If not, estimate how long it would take to systematically coach them to do the job after promotion. Would it take six months? If so, code the readiness as R1 (meaning *ready in no more than six months*). Would it take 12 months? If so, code the readiness as R2 (meaning *ready in no more than one year*).

It is not enough simply to list the people. You should also provide some justification for why you chose them. Answer this question: "Why do you think each person can be reasonably considered as a back up for the positions you identified?" If additional development is needed to prepare individuals to step up to a higher level

Exhibit 2-1. A Sample Replacement Chart

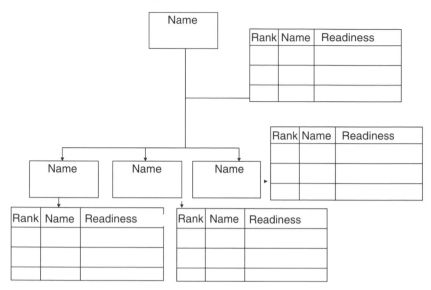

job, identify specifically what development you think they might need. For instance, "this person needs to be given coaching on how to use our budget system," or "this person needs exposure to our field sales people, who don't know her."

HOW SHOULD YOU MANAGE COMMUNICATION ABOUT REPLACEMENTS?

The most famous question in succession planning is "to tell or not to tell"—just as Hamlet soliloquized, "to be or not to be."

Generally speaking, there are advantages and disadvantages to telling or not telling people that they appear on a replacement chart. Consider the list in Exhibit 2-2.

Another option, of course, is to strike a balance. One way is to devise a "high-potential list" each year. Individuals can be told, "this

Exhibit 2-2. Should People Know They Are on a Replacement Chart?

Tell people they are on a replacement chart

Advantages	*Disadvantages*
• Can motivate individuals	• Can give people an incentive to undercut or sabotage their boss
• Can serve as a retention strategy	• Can lead to a "crown prince" or "crown princess" syndrome, in which the person sees no reason to work harder because "the promotion is guaranteed"
	• Can demotivate those who are not chosen

Do not tell people they are on a replacement chart

Advantages	*Disadvantages*
• Can leave options open of whom to choose when the time comes	• Can lead to turnover of top performers who see no future for themselves
• Will preserve the motivation of those not chosen	• People may see no reason to prepare for the future or develop themselves for higher level responsibility

year you are on the high-potential list." But they can also be told that the list will be reviewed each year and that their status could change if their performance diminishes, if their efforts to develop themselves diminish, or if business needs for talent change. While that approach does not "guarantee" promotion, it is a balanced approach. After all, business conditions may change through no fault of individuals, and their status may change as a result of a merger, an acquisition, a company bankruptcy, a recession, or other major organizational changes.

One thing is important: *Don't promise what you can't deliver.* In addition, be careful whom you tell, when you tell them, and how you tell them. "To tell or not to tell" sounds like a "one-size-fits-all" approach. But managers may choose to tell an individual selectively, even when not telling is the organization's norm. That may be done as a surgical strike to retain a key performer. If you hear that a top performer is looking for another job, you may want to talk to your own boss and HR people about "telling" as a means of retaining.

And, if you do tell, be careful about *how* you tell. Avoid making blanket promises (for example, "you are going to be my successor," which sounds like an absolutely guaranteed decision). Remember that it is possible to make an oral contract that could be enforceable in a court despite dramatic changes in business conditions over time that might necessitate alternative replacements.

HOW CAN YOU ACT ON THE INFORMATION YOU OBTAIN FROM REPLACEMENT CHARTING?

A major advantage of replacement charting is that it can give you and other managers a more realistic sense of your organization's—or your department's—bench strength. How many people can reasonably be considered as back ups for key positions? If they are scarce, then that can serve the same purpose as any other inventory by showing when it may be necessary to hire additional staff to develop as replacements. If that is not done, then it is fair to ask how long it might take to find a suitable, well-qualified replacement if an off-the-street hire is necessary. The biggest problem is the lag time needed to fill a vacancy from outside the organization. That can be a very long time in an emergency! And even if suitable replacements can be recruited, they may have trouble "fitting in" or becoming instantly productive.

GROOMING A REPLACEMENT

Grooming a replacement does not mean sending the person off to a training program. Since 90 percent of development occurs on the job, your challenge as manager is to figure out how to groom people where they are. As in most other business activities, a plan is in order.

A good approach is to start by listing everything you do on a daily and then a weekly basis. It must be more detailed than a typical job description. Try to make it comprehensive, more like a log of your activities than a job description. (Use the worksheet in Exhibit 2–3 if it is helpful.) Then, think about whether there a natural starting point? Should some things be introduced first because they logically come before others?

Once you have assembled that list in the proper order, decide how to do it, when to do it, and how to check that your approach to grooming a person is actually working.

When this plan is prepared, sit down and review it with the people you are grooming. Explain what you are doing. Avoid promising a promotion, but do indicate that you are embarking on an effort to develop people to serve as back ups in case of emergency. Then, ask them if they are willing to go through this development process. Avoid arm-twisting at all cost. You want to find people who will buy into the plan. You may also be able to determine if individuals have a desire to be promoted. Most organizations do not determine if individuals want to be promoted, but many people in today's organizations actually do not want a promotion, even if offered. They may have an idea about the pay raise they would get,

(*text continued on page 25*)

Exhibit 2-3. What Do You Do on a Daily Basis?

Directions: If you are trying to groom a successor, you need to have a plan of attack. It starts by being very clear about what you do on a daily, weekly, and monthly basis. Start by brainstorming everything you can think of that you do on a daily basis. Make it as complete as possible. If it is more helpful, keep a log of all of your activities on a daily basis. Then add in any especially critical things that you do periodically. *Use whatever might be helpful below.* Part I focuses on as many typical work activities that you can think of that you perform on a daily basis. Part II focuses on any especially critical or important work activities that you perform periodically—but perhaps not every day. Part III can be a log of your average week, completed hour by hour.

Part I. Your Brainstormed List of Typical Work Activities

What are the most important activities that you perform on a daily basis? (Make a list and try to make it as comprehensive as possible)

Part II. Any Especially Important Activities That You Perform Periodically (But Not Every Day)

What are the most important activities that you perform periodically? (Make a list and try to make it as comprehensive as possible)

Part III. A Log of Your Week

Monday	
9 a.m.	
10 a.m.	
11 a.m.	
12 noon	
1 p.m.	
2 p.m.	
3 p.m.	
4 p.m.	
5 p.m.	
Tuesday	
9 a.m.	
10 a.m.	
11 a.m.	
12 noon	
1 p.m.	
2 p.m.	
3 p.m.	
4 p.m.	
5 p.m.	
Wednesday	
9 a.m.	
10 a.m.	
11 a.m.	
12 noon	
1 p.m.	
2 p.m.	
3 p.m.	
4 p.m.	
5 p.m.	

(*continued*)

Exhibit 2-3. Continued

Thursday	
9 a.m.	
10 a.m.	
11 a.m.	
12 noon	
1 p.m.	
2 p.m.	
3 p.m.	
4 p.m.	
5 p.m.	
Friday	
9 a.m.	
10 a.m.	
11 a.m.	
12 noon	
1 p.m.	
2 p.m.	
3 p.m.	
4 p.m.	
5 p.m.	
Other Days/Times-Your Notes	

and it is not appealing when they consider how much more work they may have to tolerate in return. They prefer more work-life balance than a promotion might allow. By having this discussion, you will have a much better idea about the real career goals of people you identified as possible back ups.

In many cases, it is wise to identify and develop more than one back up for the simple reason that people quit, retire, transfer, or otherwise depart from the development regimen. Replacement charts typically request three back ups.

AVOIDING COMMON MISTAKES IN IDENTIFYING AND GROOMING A REPLACEMENT

Let's consider five common mistakes that should be avoided when identifying and grooming a replacement.

BILL'S TIP – RATING POTENTIAL

If you are asked to rate the potential (promotability) of your workers, there is a danger that you will be swayed by:

- *The single-asset worker:* Someone who has a major benefit, such as an employee who does an outstanding job with budgets. This person may, however, struggle to do almost anything else.
- *The highly credentialed worker:* Someone who has much education or highly desirable experience. Be careful about giving this person a special benefit of the doubt.
- *The fighting worker:* Someone who fights with you. You may be encouraged to rate the person negatively.

Avoid these temptations if asked to rate someone's promotability.

Mistake 1: The "Like-Me" Fallacy

The "like-me" fallacy is the well-known bias to choose people like yourself. Men prefer men; women prefer women; engineers prefer engineers; and graduates of the same university prefer graduates of that school. The more that someone matches you in background, the more comfortable you are with him or her—and that means you will be swayed in your judgment because you feel that person must be good.

There are, of course, at least two major problems with that logic.

One problem is that people like you may not actually be the best qualified for promotion. Sometimes high potentials are not the supervisors' favorite people. They can even be irritating to their supervisors because they ask tough questions and may even steal credit that supervisors feel they deserve because they are the head of the work unit or department.

A second problem is that, even if you are the best-qualified person for the job you are in now, that does not mean the organization will *always* need someone like you. Future competitive conditions in the business may mean that your ideal replacement could be someone so unlike you that you would actually detest them if you met them. The point is that you must overcome your personal bias and your personal comfort level and think for the business. What kind of person will be best equipped to get the results needed in your division, department, or organization in the future when that back up is really needed? That is the question to consider.

To avoid this common mistake, use more than one person when making selection—and promotion—decisions. At least get the input of other people you trust. If nothing else, talk to your spouse or significant other about it. Explain that you are seeking information to make sure that you are not engaged in "cloning yourself." To do that, think about all the reasons why someone else might be a better choice. If that is hard to do, then perhaps you have indeed made the best choice. Another way to do that is to try to make assessments of promotability—usually called "potential"—more objective by using descriptions of ideal performers based on the competencies and behaviors desired. Then assess individuals against those descriptions.

Mistake 2: The "Like-Us" Fallacy

Have you ever been on a selection team, interviewed people for a position, and heard that one applicant was "well qualified but won't fit in here?" If you have heard that someone "will not fit in here," you may have been exposed to the "like-us" fallacy. It is similar to the "like-me" fallacy"—except it is a problem at a group level.

It should be noted that if you do hear that statement in an interview, you should ask "*why* won't the person fit in here?" Listen to the answer carefully. Remember that sometimes it is a good idea to have fresh ideas and approaches that are outside the "normal way we do things here." Quantum leaps in productivity improvement rarely come from groups in which everyone looks, thinks, and acts alike.

To avoid this common mistake, seek contrary evidence. Ask people what are the worst things that could happen if someone did not fit in and what are the best things that could happen. In short, directly challenge the assumption that it is always best to choose people who will "fit in." While it is true that it is usually helpful to find someone who will get along in a given corporate culture, care must be taken with assuming that everyone must look alike and act alike to get along. That is not always necessary or even desirable.

Mistake 3: Recency Bias

Recency bias is the tendency to be swayed in decision-making by recent events. You may be tempted to form a favorable—or unfavorable—opinion about a possible back up's potential based on recent events. If a worker did an exceptionally good job or bad job lately, it can sway your overall opinion.

Avoid this common mistake by taking steps to look at overall performance over a long time span. Put recent events in perspective. One major mistake—or one outstanding example of performance— does not necessarily mean an individual is exceptionally bad or good.

Mistake 4: The Halo Effect

The halo effect is the tendency to form an overall favorable judgment based on one trait or one previous experience with an individual. It is a tendency that comes up in many forms of assessment, including decisions to choose a back up or a replacement. Managers tend not to think of people in specific terms; rather, they form overall impressions that color their opinions of others.

In a 1920 study conducted by Edward L. Thorndike, the researcher asked officers to rate their soldiers. Thorndike noticed that the ratings tended to be highly correlated. From that he concluded that ratings tend to be based on generalizations about people. In more recent times, research on personalities revealed that some characteristics tend to sway opinions more than others. As one example, physically attractive men or women tend to be given the benefit of the doubt more than average-looking people.

To avoid this common mistake, involve other people in your decision-making. You should also set out to look for contrary evidence to indicate that a person you like or that you have a good opinion of may not, in fact, be the best choice.

Mistake 5: The Horn Effect—Sometimes Called "Pigeon Holing"

The horn effect is the opposite of the halo effect. But instead of a positive overall impression, the horn effect is an overall negative impression of someone. In pigeon holing, individuals are rated according to criteria that do not accurately predict their ability. A simple example may illustrate the point.

A manager once told me that a female worker of his would never be promoted because she was "disloyal." I knew she was a 20-year veteran of the company, so I asked, "How can she be disloyal?" He replied, "Well, she has worked in 5 divisions in 20 years." I then asked, "Isn't that a good thing? She has had exposure to many parts of the business and that leads to a well-rounded view of the business. Isn't that desirable?" And he said, "No, she was disloyal to the managers she worked for because she was able to get a promotion in another department without getting her boss's approval first. In this corporate culture, that's the death penalty. She will never be promoted."

That worker was pigeon holed.

Avoid these problems by making the promotion criteria as specific, and as job-specific, as possible. Flush out any unrelated criteria and expose them for what they are. They can be red herrings that influence decisions without being particularly useful when deciding objectively if someone can perform effectively at a higher level of responsibility.

THE MANAGER'S DAILY ROLE IN MODELING VALUES AND ETHICS

The future of talent management centers as much around values *and* ethics as it does performance and potential. While many organizations today attempt to assess workers' present job performance and possible future potential for advancement, fewer make *objective* assessments of values and ethics as part of the determination of whether individuals are talented—or are promotable. And yet it would seem that ethics and values are major topics of concern today.

But what are values? What are ethics? Why are they important? What do they have to do with talent management? How are they assessed? And what should you do, as manager, in modeling values and ethics? This part of the chapter addresses these important questions.

Values Defined

A *personal value* is something that an individual believes is good or bad. Similarly, a *business value* is something that an organization's people range on a continuum from good to bad. Personal values are influenced by upbringing, national culture, and many other factors that shape an individual. Business values are influenced by the beliefs of the founders and come to be silently practiced as part of the organization's corporate culture. Business values are thus much related to what, based on the experience of the organization (its so-called *institutional memory*), are regarded as good and bad business practices.

There is a difference between *espoused values* (what we say is good or bad) and *values in use* (what we actually do). Individuals and organizational leaders may say one thing and do another. Hence, not all values guide practice.

Individuals and organizations must have compatible value systems if the people are to stay in the organization. Strong corporate cultures have strong value systems. Sometimes those values stem from the corporate culture, and sometimes they stem from the profession that people are members of. For instance, Wal-Mart as a company has a strong corporate culture. Certain values are inherent. Likewise, the medical profession has a strong value system that stresses patient care as the highest good and that value shapes the culture of many medical institutions.

Ethics Defined

Ethics involves beliefs about what is right and wrong. Ethics does not mean the same thing as values. Consider: what is good (a value) can be right or wrong (ethics); what is bad (a value) can be right or wrong (ethics). Like values, ethics can range on a continuum from right to wrong. And there can be nearly infinite shades of gray.

If you poll a group of managers about what they think of when they think of ethics, you are likely to get a range of opinions. Some will associate ethics with what is *legal;* some will associate it with what is *moral;* some will link it to *religious beliefs;* some will think of ethics in the *context of the work they do or the profession they practice;*

and, of course, some will think of it in the very limited sense of compliance with a company's code of conduct.

Why Are Values and Ethics Important?

Public perceptions of businesses around the world have been steadily declining. Small wonder! In the last 10 years, most of the Fortune 500 companies have been involved in at least one ethics scandal. Widely publicized debacles—such as those

BILL'S TIP – ETHICS
Ethics is not something separate from daily work but rather should be integrated with it. It is manifest in behavior. As a manager, you are the model of ethics for workers. Watch your step! Talk about ethical dilemmas as they come up and ask workers for their opinions on how to handle them. That will give you a chance to assess their ethics.

affecting Enron, Global Crossing, Worldcom (and more recently Lehman Brothers, AIG, and Merrill Lynch)—have done little to improve the image of business. And the financial bailout of Wall Street has not improved that image when, for instance, it was reported that executives leading their companies into bankruptcy were rewarded lavishly with stock options and performance bonuses. Despite public relations and lobbying efforts that are among the best, businesses still suffer from an "image problem" as companies "downsize" to save money while giving their CEOs huge bonuses for purported good performance or retention. In good economic times, business enjoys a favorable image; in bad economic times, business experiences a tarnished image.

Values and ethics are important because what people believe is good and bad or right and wrong does matter. What you believe matters. And what company leaders believe matters.

If the public does not trust business to be good or to do the right thing, then the government will step in and increase regulation

---

BILL'S TIP - ETHICS

Ethics matter. According to a study conducted by the Ethics Resource Center, one in three workers have observed ethical misconduct in their organizations within the last three years. More specifically:

- 26 percent saw lying to employees or customers.
- 25 percent saw information intentionally withheld.
- 24 percent witnessed abusive behavior toward employees.
- 21 percent saw workers reporting their hours improperly.

---

and oversight laws. Business leaders may cry foul after an onerous law like Sarbanes-Oxley is enacted. But, let's face it: they made their beds and must lie in them. If business cannot police itself, then the public will demand that government do so.

In the future, it will be even more important that business set a positive example. Businesses must not only *be* good and right, but they must also be *perceived* as good and right. And that requires a long-term commitment for business leaders to say what they mean and mean what they say—to walk the walk as well as talk the talk.

What Do Values and Ethics Have to Do with Talent Management?

The future of a business is shaped not just by its strategy but by the values, ethics, and ability of its leaders. For that reason, values and ethics are foundational issues in talent management. They are at least as important as competencies, which are the characteristics associated with performance. And yet they are rarely considered in assessing an employee's potential for future promotion.

It is no wonder that organizations tend to promote those who are good at performing. The problem is that there is, and should be, more to it than just performance and potential in determining promotability.

Individual and organizational values and ethics are also important issues that must be increasingly considered when deciding who to promote into leadership positions. Consider such issues as these:

- What does an individual value?
- What does the individual believe is good or bad, and why?
- What does the individual believe is ethical and unethical?
- What does the organization value?
- On what basis does the organization reward and punish?
- How does an organization recognize and reward ethical and values-related achievement?
- How do the organization's leaders respond to ethical dilemmas? Value dilemmas?
- How should future organizational leaders respond to ethical dilemmas? Value dilemmas?
- How are ethics and values addressed in recruiting, developing, and retaining talented people?

Assessing Values and Ethics

Much has been written on values clarification, and ethics has also been a major focus of attention. Despite this, much of what has been done in these areas remains out of reach for typical managers. In short, they are difficult to apply and assess a practical result from in a daily business environment. While many instruments exist to measure values and ethics, their use seems suspect.

What You Should Do to Model Values and Ethics

As a manager, you are a role model. Others watch you closely. They watch what you do on and off the job. And secrets are hard to keep.

People also draw conclusions about what you value and what you believe is ethical based on your behavior and comments.

If you are frustrated and belittle a customer to a worker, then the worker is "hearing" more than you realize. You have set an example that it is all right to belittle customers. If you are angry at a worker and belittle him or her publicly in a meeting, other people see what you did—and draw a conclusion about the kind of person you are. If you use sarcasm, other people hear it and grow uncomfortable around you. If you belittle one worker to others, then everyone will worry that you talk behind people's backs. Even if you have problems with alcohol or drug use, workers may regard that as a role model for what it takes to be successful. In short, no matter what you do—and what excuse or mitigating factor may exist for it—you are setting an example.

Your most talented workers are among those who see the example you set. And they naturally draw the conclusion that if you are a leader and you are doing something, it must be something good. You teach by example more than by what you say.

For that reason, you should give careful thought to your daily behavior—and especially how you behave in front of the possible future leaders of the organization. You are establishing the cultural norm for what is good and bad and right and wrong.

APPLICATION QUESTIONS

1. One of the author's consulting clients sent out an e-mail to his managers asking each to identify up to three people who would be their back ups in case of emergency. Assume you were asked the same question by your supervisor. How would you answer it? On what basis do you believe some people are more qualified than others to be your back ups in case of emergency? How many names could you list?

2. Prepare a detailed, specific description of your job. Try to list everything you do in as much detail as possible. Then identify about three people from your own area of responsibility who could serve as short-term OR long-term back ups in case you suddenly became ill. For each person, identify which tasks on your job list each of them can already do and which each of them needs further development to perform. Then create an an action plan for each person that indicates when and how you will "show them the ropes."

3. Assume for a moment that you work in a small department and have nobody you could name as an emergency back up. What advice would you give your own supervisor about what he or she should do in case of emergency?

4. One problem with replacement planning, as it is described in this chapter, is that it traditionally assumes that the organization chart will remain stable. And, yet, many senior executives say they would handle an emergency loss of talent by combining work groups. What managers in your organization could take over your duties in case of an emergency? List them and then describe what you believe they would absolutely need to know that they may not already know about what you do?

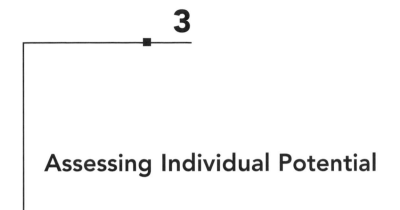

Assessing Individual Potential

How do you recognize an individual with potential? In other words, how do you know that someone has the potential to be promoted? And, given the importance of talent and how quickly things move in the business world, potential should be recognized as soon as possible—not in *years* but in *weeks*.

WHAT NOT TO DO WHEN ASSESSING POTENTIAL

Perhaps it helps to begin by describing what not to do. About 60 percent of U.S. companies have no specific way, beyond performance management systems, to rate an individual's current work performance or assess an individual's potential for promotion. Managers in these organizations assume that if workers can perform successfully in their current jobs, they are *guaranteed* to be successful in higher level jobs.

To be sure, it is a well-known principle of employee selection that the best way to predict future performance is to examine past performance. That is why so much time is spent on job applications, background checks, and employment interviews. But is that principle *always* true?

Consider the flip side, which is the assumption that success at one level on an organization chart should be rewarded with a promotion to higher levels of responsibility on the chart. This leads to the well-known *Peter Principle,* described by Dr. Laurence J. Peter and Raymond Hull in *The Peter Principle* (1968). The *Peter Principle* states that members of an organization are rewarded with promotions as long as they work competently. But eventually they are promoted to a level at which they cannot perform—and they get stuck there. And, "*Peter's Corollary* states that 'in time, every post tends to be occupied by an employee who is incompetent to carry out his duties' and adds that [most real] 'work is accomplished by those employees who have not yet reached their level of incompetence.'"

Of course, one troublesome fact is that performing at higher levels of responsibility is *different* from performing at current levels. Past success may be a predictor of future success if all else is equal. But in promotion decisions, the past is not necessarily the best indicator of the future. Why? Because the level of responsibility and work duties may be quite different. In short, it is tough to know how well individuals can perform if their performance at higher levels of responsibility has never been observed.

Some Thoughts on What to Do to Assess Potential for Promotion

Consider this analogy of an individual's ability to ride a bike with an individual's ability to perform a higher level job. How do you know if people can ride bicycles if you have never seen them do it?

One way to find out if people can ride bicycles is to ask their immediate supervisors. That is akin to asking managers which employee should be promoted. Unfortunately, as noted in the previous chapter, that approach can be influenced by the so-called "like-me" bias, in which individuals tend to pick people like themselves when called upon to make a selection or promotion decision. In short, manager nominations can lead to cloning. Managers who can ride bicycyles may assume that people they like, and are thus like themselves, can also ride a bike. The problem is like that of the classic problem confronting a teacher, who may assume that because they know something other people will also know it.

A second way to find out if people can ride bicycles is to ask many people, such as their immediate supervisors, peers, and subordinates. That is like conducting a 360-degree assessment. After the results are in, you know what others perceive—but you still don't know for sure if people can really ride bicycles. Pooled ignorance is no substitute for observed performance.

A third way is to put people on stationary bicycles like those found in fitness centers. Ask those who have ridden bicycles to observe how well people can ride and rate their abilities. That is similar to an assessment center, which consists of simulated work at a higher level responsibility. While this approach can assess the raters' perceptions of the individuals' abilities to function in a simulation, it still does not really address whether people can actually ride a bicycle on the street.

A fourth way is to ask people to produce work results at the same level as their immediate supervisors. That will probably require coaching by immediate supervisors. When the results are in, the raters will see the quality of the work—but won't know how much of it was done by the individuals and how much by their supervisors.

A fifth way is to ask individuals to participate in realistic tryouts. This is the most effective. The same principle should be applied to promotions. In tryouts, individuals assume the duties of their immediate supervisors on a short-term basis. It is like putting people on bicycles and giving them a shove to find out if they can ride. But few organizations do that, even though doing so would not seem to be difficult. Of course, after the job tryout is completed, the individual and her immediate supervisor should *formally assess* how well the individual performed at that higher level. Both the individual and the organization would thus have a basis for making better promotion, and development, decisions.

ASSESSING POTENTIAL ON A DAILY BASIS

How should managers assess potential on a daily basis? Consider these possibilities

Grooming Approach 1: A "Stretch" Project Challenge

One way to test and develop the potential of individuals is to offer them a challenge that goes beyond the skills you have seen them previously demonstrate. As a simple example, pick one activity from your own job description and delegate it for a specific time span to those you want to assess and develop. Sit the people down and explain that you are going to challenge them. Detail what they are to do, how they should do it, and how you will check on them, and show them good and bad examples (if possible).

Take care with this approach. You will need to manage expectations, avoiding promises of promotions or pay raises. Simply say that you are trying to see how well they can meet a challenge. Note for how long you will challenge them. Take back the activity when the time comes. Give detailed feedback on how well the people performed.

Grooming Approach 2: An Action Learning Project

A second way to assess and develop people is to use action learning, which involves learning while doing. First associated with classroom-based case studies in executive education, action learning has recently expanded to on-the-job experiences.

Start with a real business problem. Form a cross-functional team of people who have the ability to solve the problem through full-time or part-time project work. Choose people who could benefit from cross-functional exposure, perhaps because they have rarely strayed out of their silos. Unlike classroom training, which usually does not have consequences for failure, an action learning project has real stakes. Failure could affect the individual's pay raise and chances of promotion. Team members work together to investigate the problem, propose solutions, experiment with possible solutions, and meet expectations for improvement.

Action learning is especially useful in broadening the cross-functional exposure of individuals. At the same time, team members have a chance to learn about the business while tackling a real problem—and perhaps one with such high visibility that it will put them under the scrutiny of senior decision-makers. If the team solves the problem, the members share credit; if the team fails, the members share the blame. That puts teeth in the development process in a way that is rarely true in classroom-based training experiences.

Grooming Approach 3: Delegate Your Responsibilities

A third way to assess and develop people is to delegate a "chunk" of your work responsibilities to an individual you would like to assess and/or develop. This approach is similar to grooming approach 1— except that, instead of giving people responsibility for *only one* of your work activities, you do so for *a group of activities*.

Suppose you took your own job description, updated it, and listed what you do as comprehensively as possible. Then you reorganized the list, with the most difficult activities to perform at the top and the less difficult activities at the bottom. You draw a line between the top and bottom. You delegate the "easier" half of your job description to the person or persons whose potential you wish to assess and develop. Coach them so that they learn how to do all the work on the "easier" half of the list. When they have demonstrated the ability to do all the "easier" activities, you take responsibility for the easier part of your duties and coach them on how to perform the more difficult part of the list. If they succeed, you have assessed and developed people to be your back ups—and possible successors—in a very practical way.

Along the way you will also need to manage individual expectations. Make clear how they should handle their current job duties while learning yours. It is advisable to hand off the person's duties to someone else if possible—and that is a chance to develop someone for *those* duties, assuming you have sufficient staff to do so.

Grooming Approach 4: A Rotational Challenge

Job rotations are well-known approaches to exposing individuals to other parts of the organization. It is also a way to test promising people in other venues as well as to develop their competencies. That may be well worth doing if you are concerned that your opinions of people have been colored by the "like-me" bias. By sending people out of your area, you may give people the chance to be observed, assessed, and developed by others.

Consider carefully, before you propose a job rotation. *Why* are you sending people on the rotation? Make clear what people should learn by the time the rotation is completed. Try to find ways to measure that, too. Be sure to ask for an opinion from the manager who oversees the duties of rotating people to give you formal and informal feedback on how well these reassigned individuals are performing.

Grooming Approach 5: Challenge Workers with a Charity or Community Group

Your organization may not easily share people across silos. But a fifth way to assess and develop individuals is to send them out of the organization for a while to a more challenging opportunity with a local charitable organization or community group. Make sure that the job is not at the same level but rather at a higher level of responsibility than the person occupies in your organization. That way, a "test" can be carried out in a way that will minimize the impact of mistakes made in your organization while people are learning.

Manage such "released-time" assignments the same way you would job rotations. Rotations do not have to be full time. In fact, you may have selected people work part time in your organization and part time in the charitable organization or community group. That way, the person is at hand to provide constant feedback about "how things are going." It will also give you a chance to "coach along the way." As a condition of the released time, the leaders of the charitable organization or community group should agree to provide detailed, formal feedback on how well people perform. That information is valuable evidence as to whether people could or could not perform well at higher levels of responsibility. The experience may also provide useful information about the individual's development needs for the future.

Grooming Approach 6: Visibility with Higher Level Management

A sixth way to assess and develop individuals is by exposing them to higher level managers. That visibility may be informal—such as including your promising people in invitations to dinner or to golf—or formal—such as including them when you deliver an oral report to the senior executive team or the board of directors.

The goal of giving people visibility is to put them in front of others. That will naturally prompt curiosity and focus attention on them. There is reluctance to promote people who are utterly unknown to the organization's leaders. Take steps to make these people known.

Higher level managers will watch them and provide informal or formal feedback about what they think. That information can be helpful or hurtful. Of course, not everything you are told needs to be fed back to the person in providing guidance. (I once had managers complain about the "whiny voice" of one of my subordinates. It would seem to be difficult to cure a perception of a "whiny voice!")

Grooming Approach 7: Visibility with Customers, Suppliers, and Distributors

A seventh way to assess and develop individuals is to give them visibility to other key stakeholder groups in the organization. That serves the same purpose as grooming approach 6, except that customers, suppliers, and distributors may have very different expectations than do the leaders of your own organization. The feedback they provide may also yield valuable clues about how promotable individuals may be—and what development needs those people may need to address before being assessed as "ready now."

Grooming Approach 8: A Short-Term Tryout

An eighth way to assess and develop individuals is to give them a short-term job tryout. Unlike grooming approaches 1 or 3, this one requires that the individual perform an *entire job* at a higher level, but the timeframe should be kept short (no more than two to three weeks). For example, the department manager is out sick for three days. One of her key reports is given the job for that time span. When the department manager returns, a formal assessment can be done to determine how well the individual performed the boss's job during the short-term tryout. The lengthiest duration would generally coincide with the maximum vacation time that managers are permitted to take based on their years of experience.

As with other methods, care must be taken to communicate how the individual's typical job duties should be handled while the person is performing the short-term tryout. As in less robust approaches, it would be advisable to let the person focus on the higher level responsibilities that will truly "test" his or her abilities and provide grist for the mill on how to develop them.

Grooming Approach 9: A Long-Term Tryout

A long-term job tryout is a ninth way to assess potential and develop individuals. A long-term job tryout would be appropriate, for example, when a manager is out on long-term disability, is on family medical leave, or is otherwise indisposed for a period longer than four weeks. An individual is promoted to "acting manager" or "acting executive" for the duration of the job incumbent's absence. His or her normal job activities at a lower level are absorbed by others. That leaves the person free to tackle new learning and develop new and more challenging competencies at that higher level of responsibility. Some organizations may choose to pay people in a way commensurate with the higher level job duties. A performance bonus may also be given if people successfully complete the assignment.

Grooming Approach 10: Combine One
or More of Grooming Approaches 1-9

A tenth way to assess and develop potential is to combine one or more of the nine approaches listed above. In short, it is not necessary (or even desirable) to choose only one way to assess and develop a person. More evidence results in better, and more objective, decisions about who is promotable and how development needs should be met.

Use Exhibit 3–1 as a worksheet to organize your thinking about which individuals to develop, what competencies you feel they may need to build, what learning projects or approaches you will use to develop them, and how you will track or evaluate the results.

Exhibit 3-1. A Worksheet to Guide Employee Development

Directions: Use this worksheet to guide your thinking on which individuals to develop, what competencies you feel they may need to develop, what learning projects or approaches you will use to develop them, and how you will track or evaluate the results. Fill out the worksheet below and review it periodically. Feel free to modify this worksheet or add spaces, as necessary, to meet any special needs that your department or work group should address.

Individuals in Your Department or Work Group	What Competencies Do They Need to Develop or What Do They Need to Learn About?	What Learning Projects, Approaches, or Experiences Will You Use to Development Them?	How Will You Track or Evaluate the Results of the Developmental Experiences?
1			
2			
3			
4			
5			
6			
7			
8			
9			
10			
11			
12			

APPLICATION QUESTIONS

1. It could be said that the ability to assess promotion potential is the essence of succession planning. Explain why that may or may not be true.

2. Everyone takes sick days and vacation time. Even you, as manager, probably do so—even though research in the United States indicates that the average manager works well beyond the traditional 40-hour work week. How do you handle emergencies that come up while you are out? Do you give the organization your cell phone number and tell them to call even when you are out sick or on vacation? Or, do you assign someone to be the "acting manager" in your stead? If you don't do it, why not? If you choose to do it, how do you give people feedback on how well they performed in the acting capacity, so that their skills can be developed for the future?

3. Create a chart to indicate who is the back up in case of emergency for *every person* in your work unit, department, or division. How many of these people are really able to carry out the work of those they back up? What cross-training plans have you put in place so that you always have trained back ups in case of emergency?

4. The chapter lists a number of ways that can be used to assess promotion potential. Can you think of any others? If so, what are they? How often have they been used in your organization? In your work unit, department, or division?

4

Recruiting and Selecting Talented People

Recruitment is the process of sourcing as many well-qualified individuals as possible to fill a vacancy or a job in an organization. Recruitment may be carried out to meet an immediate need—such as filling a specific vacancy—or carried out to reduce the time it takes to fill any position by maintaining standing lists of possible applicants to examine whenever vacancies occur.

Selection is the process of identifying the best-qualified individual to fill a vacancy. It involves comparing an individual's qualifications against the work requirements of a specific position. It may involve many steps, including completion of a job application, participation in one or more interviews, employment tests, drug tests, reference or background checks, and other ways to narrow down the list of people to the successful applicant.

THE RECRUITING AND SELECTION PROCESS

Typically, the recruiting and selection process is a series of steps. They may vary, but the general logic is that recruitment should result in a robust list of well-qualified people, the more the better, and selection should narrow that list down to the best person for the position. This approach is sometimes called the *hurdle approach,* which means that applicants must leap over a series of increasingly difficult obstacles to be selected.

One way to think about it is as follows:

- Review and update the job description.
- Clarify priorities.
- Prepare a list of criteria by which you can assess applicants consistently.
- Check existing external and internal lists or databases for possible applicants.
- Post the opening through internal job posting.
- List the opening through external recruiting channels.
- Develop an expanded list of internal and/or external applicants.
- Ask all applicants to complete applications so you can organize and compare the material about all the candidates.
- Compare applications to the listed criteria.
- Narrow down the list of applicants to only the most qualified.
- Check finalists' backgrounds, references, and credentials.
- Brief/train interviewers.
- Perform first-round employment interviews with the finalists.
- Administer job performance-related employment tests to finalists.
- Rank the finalists.
- Perform second-round employment interviews with the remaining finalists.
- Debrief candidates after each interview.
- Debrief the manager after the interviews.
- Consider what should be in an employment offer.
- Make the employment offer, contingent on successful passing of a drug test if required.
- Administer test(s).

- Reconcile any differences in the employment offer with the most successful applicant and arrange a starting date.
- If the offer is rejected by the preferred applicant, move to the next successful applicant until the employment offer is accepted by a well-qualified applicant.
- Once the offer is accepted, contact unsuccessful applicants to make them aware of the selection decision.
- Manage the onboarding process of new hires to ensure that they know the organization, division, department, and work requirements and are made to feel welcome in the organization.

These and related steps are described in more detail below. Of course, the actual process in your organization may vary from this list. If it takes longer to fill positions than you think it should, then perhaps it may be worth conducting a process improvement effort to determine all the steps in the recruiting and selection process in your organization and what makes the recruiting and selection process take so long.

BILL'S TIP – RECRUITING

You can do your job and also take steps to do recruiting. Here are some ideas:

- Get to know people who can help you in recruiting, such as thought leaders and professors.
- Build professional networks and use them to your advantage in recruiting.
- Send out e-mail blasts to your social network when you need help filling a key spot.
- Find out what applicants say they want by asking them to describe their dream position.
- Involve your workers in recruiting and tap into their social networks to advantage.

As you read the following steps, think about how you could contribute at each step. Consider what you are presently doing—and what you could or should be doing.

STEPS IN THE PROCESS

Step 1: Compare the Staffing of the Organization to the Organization's Strategic Objectives

Few organizations undertake this first step. Called *work force planning,* this step establishes staffing goals based on the organization's strategic objectives. It requires at least an annual review of how many and what kind of people are already employed by the organization (supply) compared with the number and type of people required to achieve desired results (demand). More than focused on headcount, it gives due consideration to the numbers needed to replace retiring individuals, add people for business growth or continuity, and modify existing staffing to ensure a better match between the collective competencies of the organization's work force and the work force talent needed to achieve strategic objectives.

Step 2: Review and Update Job Descriptions and Establish Competency Models

Few organizations regularly update all *job descriptions,* which literally describe the work to be done. In most cases, job descriptions are only updated when a vacancy occurs, and you have been given authorization to fill the position. At that point, you, as manager, may have to prepare an updated job description and a job requisition. While that may work fine for new positions, it is not always adequate when an existing position needs to be filled.

One reason why job descriptions are inadequate is that you are not always in the best position to know what your own workers do. In reality, the workers are often the best judges. Research suggests that when managers and their immediate reports draft job descriptions separately, they may disagree by as much as *50 percent* on the number of work activities and their relative importance. A better approach is for you and a worker to separately prepare a draft job description and then iron out disagreements so that the description is properly attuned to your different perspectives. Another reason why job descriptions are inadequate is that they are often incomplete, leaving out the full range of work activities. You should consult existing information—such as Web sites that provide government-written job descriptions—that provide an excellent starting point for customizing job descriptions to the needs of a particular corporate culture. (See, for instance, http://www.stepfour.com/genie/ and also http://online.onetcenter.org/.)

Competency models are also needed. They describe the *kind of people* who are successful, or outstanding, in doing the work. Unlike activity-oriented job descriptions, competency models should be based on the results desired and then traced back to the individual characteristics required to achieve those results.

While you may question the need for job descriptions or competency models, it is important to understand that it is not possible to source the best people to do the work when the nature of the work—and the nature of the people who are most productive in doing the work—is unclear. (If you don't know what you want, or you don't communicate it, then you don't know what you'll get!)

Competency models come in two types. *Generic competency models* focus on the common characteristics of people at the same level on the organization chart. As an example, all corporate vice presidents should share some personal characteristics in common because they occupy the same horizontal position on the organization chart. But *technical or functional competency models* are focused on the special work done in each department. They are particular to each silo on the organization chart—such as technical competencies specific to MIS, HR, accounting, or other department.

While there are many ways to conduct competency modeling, one approach is to study the people who are already successful at doing the work. Then write up what they share in common. Many books have been written on how to do that, and many consulting companies specialize in it.

Step 3: Clarify Priorities

What work activities and what competencies are most important now, and what work activities and what competencies are becoming more important as the organization's strategic plan is implemented? This step should answer that question. Before selection criteria can be established, you, as manager, must be clear on what you want the most.

Step 4: Prepare a List of Criteria to Assess Applicants Consistently

If you set out to fill a position but are not clear about how to evaluate all applicants consistently, you may easily be swayed by characteristics that are not specifically job related. The color of a person's hair, the scent of perfume, or the manner of dress may hurt or help different applicants. And yet, those factors may have little or nothing to do with the person's ability to do the job.

Prepare an assessment form based directly on the job description and the competency model. Make very clear what evidence you are looking for and how you will assess it. Then assign ratings to what is needed to do the job. Exhibit 4-1 is an example of such a form. Share this assessment form with others if they are to be involved in making a selection decision, so that everyone is in agreement about what evidence to look for and how to assign a rating to the evidence given. In that way, attention will be focused on job relatedness and the ability to get results. While it will not eliminate the possibility for abuse, it will help raters focus on what matters.

Exhibit 4-1. Assigning Ratings to Applicants

Directions: Use this worksheet to assign ratings to applicants. Use one sheet for each applicant. List the work activities of the job in the left column below. Then assign a numerical rating based on how well the applicant's qualifications match up to the work, giving evidence that the person can do the work. You may also pose questions at the interview about the individual's ability to do the work. Assign a numerical rating based on how well the individual answers the question at the interview and satisfies you that he or she is qualified. Use these scores:

0 = Not applicable
1 = Not at all qualified
2 = Somewhat qualified
3 = Qualified
4 = Exceptionally qualified

Name of the Applicant		Interviewer		
Date		Position Applied for		
Position/Job Requirements Listed on the Job Description or Job Posting	How Well Qualified?			
	Not applicable	Not at all qualified	Somewhat qualified	Qualified	Exceptionally qualified
1	0	1	2	3	4
2	0	1	2	3	4
3	0	1	2	3	4
4	0	1	2	3	4
5	0	1	2	3	4
6	0	1	2	3	4
7	0	1	2	3	4
8	0	1	2	3	4
9	0	1	2	3	4
10	0	1	2	3	4

Step 5: Check Existing External and Internal Lists or Databases for Possible Applicants

There are two places from which to recruit—inside and outside the organization. Organizations that are always recruiting should build lists of available applicants. In large companies, that information may be available electronically so that the databases can be searched by the keywords contained in job descriptions and competency models. Such a database can cut the time it takes to fill positions by assembling a large number of documents and having them readily available to search.

Internal recruitment typically centers on resume and job posting or management nomination systems. *Resume posting* permits individuals to post their resumes online, sometimes as part of an Intranet specific to one company. Of course, external search firms and many companies permit individuals to post their resumes on their Web sites for future examination. *Job posting,* on the other hand, allows managers to post information about their vacancies online within the company. A simple job posting policy appears in Exhibit 4–2. Compare that to the posting policy of your company.

Care should be taken with job posting programs. For one thing, you, as a manager, may not always like them because they permit employees to signal a willingness to leave the department. That may make your job more difficult, because there may be no guarantee that you will be given permission to replace a departing person or will find someone as good as the one who leaves. Another problem is that some job posting programs, particularly in unionized organizations, focus on a single criterion (such as seniority) as the only issue to be considered in a posting decision. Of course, you should want the best-qualified applicants, not just those who worked the longest for the company.

Manager nomination programs, as internal recruitment efforts, work only when you nominate people for movement. While the world would be a wonderful place if everyone were always motivated by what is best for the company, such is not always the case.

In some instances, managers may actually nominate their worst performers (or their biggest trouble makers) so as to foist them off on other, less wary, managers. Likewise, they may be unwilling to recommend their best people for fear that they may not get a replacement or may get someone who is not nearly so productive. That leads to a work setting in which managers hoard the best talent and release only the worst.

External recruitment typically focuses on identifying the best approaches to get the word out, including (in no particular order of importance or effectiveness):

Exhibit 4-2. A Sample Job Posting Policy

Purpose

A fundamental precept of [Company's] management philosophy is to develop people from within the organization to the greatest extent possible. To develop successfully as a professional, an employee must grow into and through several positions and job levels during the course of a working career. Job posting plays an essential role in identifying interested and qualified candidates for these growth opportunities. Internal job posting is considered a sound management practice aimed at reducing turnover, maintaining morale, and increasing organizational commitment by providing personal and career development opportunities to all employees. The job-posting process does not guarantee internal applicants first right of refusal, however. Our employment policy is to select the most qualified applicant from any available source. Internal applicants are given preference only in cases where job considerations and qualifications are equal.

Procedure

Job openings occur because of newly created positions, transfers, and terminations. All hiring and staffing decisions should involve a discussion between the department/operating unit manager and the Human Resources designate. Once the decision is made to post a position, the Human Resources designate is responsible for completing the Job Posting Form and distributing it to the appropriate locations. If a qualified replacement is available within the department where the opening occurs, the manager may fill the opening from within the department without posting. This, of course, often results in the replacement's job being posted. Similarly, officer vacancies/additions may or may not be posted depending on management's perception of the organization's best interests. All other positions are posted within [Company] or, in cases where officer positions are posted, throughout [Company].

Source: http://www.npmapestworld.org/management-channel/form-book/
transfer/job-posting-policy.htm
Used by permission of the Web site.

- Advertisements in newspapers, trade publications such as industry magazines, and the media (radio, television, or the company's Web site).
- Signs placed outside the organization indicating "help wanted."
- Search firms.
- On-campus recruiting.
- Special Web sites.
- Employee referrals.
- Temporary agencies.

According to a 2002 survey conducted by the Society for Human Resource Management, small firms (1-99 employees) and medium-sized firms (100-499) tend to get the best value in recruiting by focusing on employee referrals, online advertisements, and newspaper advertisements. Large firms (with more than 500 workers) get the best value from online advertisements, employee referrals, and newspapers advertisements. Some organizational leaders may also decide to add special efforts to their recruiting to attract protected class employees—including older workers, minorities, or women.

Of course, it is important to establish specific, measurable objectives to guide the organization's internal and external recruitment efforts. In short, why is the organization conducting recruitment? Rarely is it done solely to find qualified people. There are usually other objectives as well, such as improving brand awareness of the organization, improving community relations, and many other such goals. These goals should guide the approaches selected for recruitment. In additional, recruiters should track the costs of recruiting and compare them to the number and quality of leads and actual hires generated.

Step 6: Post the Opening Through Internal Job Posting

Many organizations favor a promote-from-within policy. It is felt that this policy improves employee morale and may serve as a retention strategy to keep turnover low. Of course, no organization should strive for 100 percent promote from within, because it will tend to lead to *inbreeding,* a condition in which everyone thinks alike because they were all socialized in the same corporate culture. It is good to obtain fresh ideas occasionally from outside at all levels on the organization chart.

Nevertheless, a good job posting system will be based on a policy that clarifies the goals of the effort, indicates the procedures used to guide posting, and describe how employees go about signaling interest in competing for a job vacancy in their own or other departments. Software can help make the program work, but people must administer the software. The real issue is to clarify on what basis decisions will be made about filling vacancies and how much and what kind of feedback will be given to unsuccessful internal job posting applicants. In short, should employees be told why they were not selected as a finalist to be interviewed or why they were not chosen for the position? Some organizations do not provide feedback; others require it. One advantage to doing it is to encourage individual development; one disadvantage is that it takes time and staff.

An important point to make about internal job posting is that expectations must be managed. Employees must be told repeatedly that the organization will not choose people just because they have worked in the organization for the longest time; rather, positions will always go to the best-qualified applicants. That may mean that workers who strive for promotion may need to be developed for the special competencies required at higher levels of the organization and that may mean they must participate in training or in other developmental efforts, such as job rotations.

Step 7: List the Opening Through External Recruiting Channels

How your organization recruits can influence the quality of the people attracted to apply and how quickly a vacancy can be filled with a qualified person.

The most topical issue in recruiting today is called *e-recruiting,* the term associated with using the Web and/or Internet to source applicants to fill vacancies. E-recruiting may be active or passive. *Active e-recruiting* means directly soliciting qualified individuals. *Passive e-recruiting* means trolling the Web (and other sources) for qualified individuals who may already be employed and successful, but who may represent special talent needed to meet the organization's needs.

Many Web sites exist on which organizations can post job openings or search large databases that contain the resumes of possible applicants. Some have a fee; others are free. Quick-thinking people are also experimenting with a range of topical approaches to recruiting—such as recruiting on popular social networking Web sites, like YouTube, My Face, or My Space.

Savvy managers and recruiters also know that attracting qualified talent means more than just offering what everyone else is offering. Growing interest exists in so-called employment branding, which should not be confused with the company's brand. *Employment branding* refers to the reputation that your organization has as an employer. A ranking on *Forbes Magazine's* "100 Best Companies to Work for" is essentially a placement on the list of best employment brands and that means the organization enjoys a distinct advantage when

---

BILL'S TIP – RECRUITING
You can do your job and also take steps to do recruiting. Here are some ideas:

- Determine where prospective applicants hear about your organization or opening.
- Hold an open house in your work area.
- Offer free career workshops for members of your community or for customers of your company.
- More than 52 million Americans use the Internet to search for a job. Will they find your opportunity if they look there?

attracting talented people. (For the current list of the 100 Best Companies, see http://money.cnn.com/magazines/fortune/bestcompanies/2008/full_list/.) That ranking is not arbitrary. Employees vote their employer into a rank based on criteria established by the Great Place to Work® Institute. (For a list of the criteria for a Great Place to Work®, see http://www.greatplacetowork.com/great/model.php.)

Step 8: Develop an Expanded List of Internal and/or External Applicants

The recruiting process, both internal and external, should generate a list of possible applicants. Some may already appear on existing databases; others may have been attracted by notices of a vacancy. It is, of course, necessary to compile a list and make sure that the candidates are still available and interested in the position.

Step 9: Ask All Applicants to Complete Applications to Organize the Material About All the Candidates So That Comparable Information Is Available

Some organizations simply ask applicants to submit their resumes or curriculum vitae (cv). The problem with this, however, is that not everybody supplies the same information. Some people, for instance, may not list the salary or wage they earned in previous jobs. That information may be something your organization wants to know. Other people may list unwanted information that could sway decision-making—or give the appearance of doing so. (What do you do if the people list that they are members of the American Nazi party, the Ku Klux Klan, or the Hell's Angels? Do you really need to know that? Even less controversial organizations could give some people pause, such as membership in a religious organization.)

For these reasons, it is usually best to ask all job applicants—internal and external—to fill out an application. The application can be crafted to yield only job-relevant information. Many organizations now request that applications be completed online, although it is sometimes helpful to have applicants complete the application on a terminal at your place of employment so that people who have insufficient literacy skills may be identified.

Step 10: Compare Applications to the List of Criteria

At some point—usually agreed on in advance—you, as the manager, should review the available applications and compare them to the list of criteria (prepared in advance) to see how many qualified applicants have been attracted. If not enough people have applied, then more rigorous recruiting efforts may need to be made. (For instance, ask employees to help by referring well-qualified people they know.) Sometimes a search will have a specific time span and a "closing date."

Step 11: Narrow Down the List of Applicants to the Most Qualified

Once the recruiting process yields at least three well-qualified people, take the list of all applicants and narrow it down to only those who meet all the priority requirements.

Step 12: Check Finalists' Backgrounds and Credentials

Once Step 11 is completed, carry out a background check in compliance with your organization's HR policies. This may involve verifying references, credentials, and a host of other possible facts, including criminal background records, credit history, and so forth. Of course, such checks can only be carried out if the applicants have signed an agreement in advance to permit the employer to make these checks, all of which must be conducted in compliance with existing laws, rules, and regulations of the country, state or province, and local area. These may, of course, vary.

Step 13: Brief/Train Interviewers

Managers—and anyone who conducts job interviews—should be trained to conduct selection interviews. If they have had such training, a briefing may still be helpful to remind them of "what not to ask" and "what to ask." The HR department may also provide an interview guide to ensure that all applicants are asked the same questions and that the questions asked are well documented. In that way, a paper trail is established for all interviews—and it can help to overcome "recency bias" in which the most recently interviewed applicants have an advantage because interviewers simply remember them better than they do those interviewed earlier.

Interview guides may list the exact wording to use in posing interview questions and leave room for interviewers to take notes about how applicants answered. The guides may also provide spaces for questions posed by the interviewees, as well as special questions that interviews may want to ask based on the applicant's education or work history.

Step 14: Perform First-Round Employment Interviews with the Finalists

While lower level jobs may be filled after only a few people are interviewed, jobs with more responsibility may require multiple interviews. The first interview may be undertaken to narrow down a list of finalists to one or two preferred candidates.

Step 15: Administer Job Performance-Related Employment Tests to Finalists

Applicants who jump over the first hurdle and become one of the two finalists should be given performance-related employment tests. Job tests may take many forms, of course. They may focus on biographical information, knowledge (cognitive ability), honesty (integrity tests), job knowledge, personality, physical ability, work samples, and simulations of the work.

In some cases, the test may be conducted as part of the first-round interviews. Interviews, in their own way, are also considered "tests." Simulations, as an assessment tool in job selection, appear to be on the increase (see "Use of Job Simulations Rising Steadily," *Workforce Management,* 2005, downloaded from http://www.work force.com/section/06/feature/24/18/59/index.html). Tests can be discriminatory if used improperly, and they should therefore be handled with care.

Step 16: Rank the Finalists

Once interviews and job-related tests have been completed, you can rank the finalists to determine the best candidates. At that point, the finalists may be called back for second interviews.

Step 17: Perform Second-Round Employment Interviews with the Remaining Finalists

A second interview is usually conducted to answer any questions that may remain about one or more of the finalists.

Step 18: Debrief Candidates After Each Interview

Most organizations, after each interview, inform applicants when a final decision will be made.

Step 19: Debrief the Manager After the Interviews

It is advisable to involve more than one person in selection interviews, so that the effects of the "like-me" bias are minimized. At some point, the interviewers should compare their independent scores of applicants.

Step 20: Consider What Should Be in an Employment Offer

Based on the applicant's background and salary history, it is necessary to identify what offer the organization is willing to make. The organization may already have HR policies governing this issue, and those should be consulted.

Step 21: Make the Employment Offer, Contingent on Successful Passing of Any Necessary Test(s)

Many organizations extend an employment offer but make it contingent on successful passing of some mandated tests. For instance, some employers are required to administer drug tests. Employers required to administer drug tests may vary depending on nation or jurisdiction, but since the administration of President Ronald Reagan organizations that rely on professional drivers, provide safety-essential transportation, are in the oil and gas-related industries, and work for some federal department must be tested for illegal substances.

Step 22: Administer Test(s)

Not all tests are the same. There are actually a large number of such tests. That is, for instance, true of drug tests and intelligence tests. Drug tests may screen for different substances. Employers must follow legal requirements in administering and interpreting drug test results. However, "more than three-quarters of America's 14.8 million drug users have jobs. Drug users are almost four times as likely to be involved in a workplace accident as sober workers, and five times as likely to file a workers' compensation claim, according to government data. Drug users miss more days of work, show up late, and change jobs more often. The cost of a drug test, meanwhile, is usually less than $50." In addition, "almost 6 percent of all employees randomly screened and 4 percent of job applicants typically test positive," according to the International Herald Tribune (Fahmy, D., May 10 2007, "More U.S. employers testing workers for drug use," downloaded from http://www.iht.com/articles/2007/05/10/business/drugtests.php).

Step 23: Reconcile Any Differences in the Employment Offer with the Applicant and Arrange Start Date

Once the decision is made about whom to hire, the employer may have to continue negotiation once an employment offer is made. Not all offers are immediately accepted. Employed workers may have to negotiate a starting date. Even internal moves may need time to arrange things. Negotiation on the start date is the most common issue, and that is particularly true for senior managers with significant responsibilities in their current positions. The salary offer and other employment conditions may also be subject to negotiation and that can extend the time it takes to get the worker onboard. If the worker's spouse is employed, that may also open up issues that may have to be addressed before an offer can be finalized.

Step 24: If the Offer Is Rejected, Move to the Next Successful Applicant Until the Employment Offer Is Accepted by a Well-Qualified Applicant

If negotiations in step 23 break down, it may be necessary to move on to the next finalist for the position and open negotiations with him or her. For this reason, it is not wise to send out rejection letters to all finalists before an acceptance is given.

Step 25: Once the Offer Is Accepted, Contact Unsuccessful Applicants to Make Them Aware of the Decision

Once the employment offer has been made and accepted, it is then time to get back in touch with everyone who applied. Be sure to send them a letter. Do not go into the reasons why they were not chosen, but do wish them well. Doing so is wise, since it costs little and preserves some good relations with this applicant pool. Always remember that the person chosen for the job may not work out and your organization may have to get back in touch with the unsuccessful applicants at a future time.

Step 26: Manage the Onboarding Process of New Hires to Ensure They Know the Organization, Division, Department, and Work Requirements and Are Made to Feel Welcome in the Organization

Recruiting, selecting, and onboarding are not separate efforts; rather, they are a continuum. Worker expectations and opinions about the employer are shaped at every step on that continuum. How people are treated during the recruiting and selection process will influence how they already regard the employer on the first day of work.

Still, onboarding is properly regarded as a *process* and not, as in an orientation program conducted by HR, a one-time event. Onboarding means socializing people into the organization's corporate culture. The socialization process goes on forever.

Onboarding may properly be regarded at several levels. First, how are people introduced to the organization? Second, how are people introduced to the division, department, and work team of which they are part? And, third, how are they made to feel welcome in the organization?

For purposes of talent management, you should never forget that the people most likely to resign are those who were most recently hired. It just makes sense. These people have the least to lose if they quit, since they may not know many people in the organization. Hence, their social network is limited. In additional, the most recent hires probably still have resumes and applications floating around from their recent job search, and other employers may still call them. They may simply land better offers after they come to work for your organization.

What can be done about onboarding? First, workers should be given well-organized training. It should start *before* they arrive on the first day, anticipating their needs. (For instance, what does a new hire need to know before the first day of work? What about "where to park?" and "Who is the person's immediate supervisor?") Second, workers should be made to feel welcome. An effective way to do that is to assign each new hire a "peer mentor" whose job is not training but socializing. The "peer mentor" should be tasked to take new hires out for lunch for the first few days, introduce them to other people in ways that go beyond superficial handshakes, and generally make them feel that the organization is glad to have them.

Some very innovative approaches have been done during onboarding efforts. In one organization—a large company—the CEO personally gives new hires an hour's presentation and gets to know them by name! Such efforts go beyond merely signing paperwork and make new hires feel critically important to the organization.

Consult Exhibit 4–3 for a checklist to guide you, as a starting point, for developing an onboarding checklist.

Exhibit 4-3. A Sample Onboarding Checklist

A Checksheet to Guide New Staff Member Orientation	
Staff Member's Name	**Today's Date**
Trainer's Name	
Orientation Plan	
Notes on the Orientation Plan *(Make notes here about special issues for the orientation of this staff member):*	

Needed?		Questions to Answer in the Orientation			What Instructional Objectives, Activities, and Timetables Should Be Worked out to Address These Questions?
Yes ☐	No ☐	Should the New Staff Member:			
☐	☐	1		Tour company facilities, including:	
☐	☐		A	All departments?	
☐	☐		B	His/her work unit?	
☐	☐		C	Cafeteria?	
☐	☐	2		Receive a standard orientation for all new staff members, including a description of	
☐	☐		A	Employee benefits?	
☐	☐		B	Vacation time policies and scheduling?	
☐	☐		C	Holidays?	
☐	☐		D	A probationary period (if applicable)?	
☐	☐		E	Company tuition refund policy?	
☐	☐		F	Company-sponsored in-house training for staff members?	
☐	☐		G	Retirement benefits?	
☐	☐		H	Credit union?	
☐	☐		I	Off-the-job, company-sponsored social activities?	
☐	☐		J	Hours of work (starting time, lunch period, quitting time?)	
☐	☐		K	Pay periods?	
☐	☐		L	Parking arrangements?	
☐	☐		M	Other matters? (*List them below:*)	
☐	☐	3		Receive an orientation to the company, including discussion about its:	
☐	☐		A	Purpose (What is the business?)	
☐	☐		B	Goals/objectives (What is the company trying to achieve over the next five years? One year?)	
☐	☐		C	Structure (What are the departments and work units in the company? What do they do? An organization chart would be helpful for this.)	
☐	☐		D	History (How did the company get where it is today?)	

(continued)

Exhibit 4-3. Continued

Needed?		Questions to Answer in the Orientation		What Instructional Objectives, Activities, and Timetables Should Be Worked out to Address These Questions?
Yes ☐	No ☐	Should the New Staff Member:		
☐	☐	E	Top management team members (Who are they? What do they consider important?)	
☐	☐	F	Other matters? (List below)	
☐	☐	4	Receive an orientation to the department, including discussions about:	
☐	☐	A	The staff member's unit within the structure of the department?	
☐	☐	B	The department's place in the organization?	
☐	☐	C	Department goals/objectives?	
☐	☐	D	Department history?	
☐	☐	E	Other units and staff members in the department and what they do?	
☐	☐	F	The department manager's expectations for all staff members?	
☐	☐	G	What kinds of problems to bring to the department manager's attention?	
☐	☐	H	Other matters? (List them below.)	
☐	☐	5	Receive a special orientation to the new work unit, including	
☐	☐	A	A tour of the unit, with emphasis on	
☐	☐	1	The new staff member's work area?	
☐	☐	2	Washrooms?	
☐	☐	3	Copy machines?	
☐	☐	4	Vending machines?	
☐	☐	5	Computers and computer systems?	
☐	☐	6	Work stations of subordinates?	
☐	☐	B	Introductions to each staff member?	
☐	☐	C	A review of each subordinate's personnel records?	
☐	☐	D	Overview of work unit activities, tasks, and procedures?	
☐	☐	E	Overview of equipment used in the work unit?	

☐	☐		F	Overview of special procedures, if any, applicable to the work unit?	
☐	☐		G	A description of the work unit's purpose and other work units that depend on it?	
☐	☐		H	Goals/objectives of the work unit?	
☐	☐		I	History of the work unit, including special problems unique to it?	
☐	☐		J	Other matters? (List below.)	
☐	☐	6		Receive a special orientation to the job, including	
☐	☐		A	A description of what staff members do in general? (the staff member's role)	
☐	☐		B	A description of what staff members are expected to do in this company in particular?	
☐	☐		C	A review of the staff member's job description with the department manager with special emphasis on the most important duties, activities, tasks, and responsibilities of the position? (A copy of the staff member's job description will be needed for this.)	
☐	☐		D	A review of the staff member performance appraisal with special emphasis on how the staff member is evaluated and what is weighted most heavily in decisions about pay increases and promotions?	
☐	☐		E	Other matters? (List them below.)	
☐	☐	7		Receive a special review of important industry issues, including	
☐	☐		A	A discussion of what industry issues have been important in the past? Are very important at present? Are likely to become more important in the future?	
☐	☐		B	A discussion of what industry issues are likely to affect the company?	
☐	☐		C	A discussion of what industry issues are likely to affect the department?	
☐	☐		D	A discussion of what industry issues are likely to affect the staff member's work unit—and why?	
☐	☐		E	A discussion of what industry issues are likely to affect the staff member's job? The jobs of subordinates?	
☐	☐		F	Other matters? (List them below.)	
☐	☐	8		Receive details about company policies and procedures affecting the staff member's job, including hands-on training on	

(continued)

Exhibit 4-3. Continued

Needed? Yes □	Needed? No □	Questions to Answer in the Orientation		What Instructional Objectives, Activities, and Timetables Should Be Worked out to Address These Questions?
			Should the New Staff Member:	
□	□	A	Company and department planning activities?	
□	□	B	Company and department budgeting activities?	
□	□	C	Travel policies/procedures?	
□	□	D	Purchasing?	
□	□	E	Contracting for assistance?	
□	□	F	Company accounting methods?	
□	□	G	Company production control and scheduling?	
□	□	H	Company production reporting?	
□	□	I	Property control and inventory?	
□	□	J	Computer systems?	
□	□	K	Security?	
□	□	L	Personnel matters—including hiring, evaluating, disciplining and terminating subordinates?	
□	□	M	Attendance records on staff members?	
□	□	N	Phones?	
□	□	O	Other important company policies? (List them in the space below.)	
□	□	9	Receive information about federal, state, and local laws, rules and regulations affecting	
□	□	A	The industry? (for instance, regulatory bodies dealing with industry)	
□	□	B	The company? (for instance, OSHA, EEOC, and state government counterparts)	
□	□	C	The facility? (local plant or office as opposed to the entire firm)	
□	□	D	The department?	
□	□	E	The work unit?	
□	□	F	The staff member's job?	
□	□	G	Other matters? (List them below.)	

10	*Summarize on a separate sheet the instructional objectives for the new staff member's orientation. When he or she finishes the orientation, he or she should be able to:*
11	*Summarize below the activities that need to be carried out to meet each orientation objective established in question 10 above.*
12	*Summarize below the timetable for meeting the objectives and carrying out the orientation activities you decided on.*

WHAT SHOULD THE HR DEPARTMENT DO TO RECRUIT AND SELECT TALENTED PEOPLE FOR THE ORGANIZATION?

In many organizations, the HR department is expected to do most of the "heavy lifting" in the recruiting process. Consider the list of steps in the previous section. How many of those steps do you think HR should do alone? How many do you think HR should do in partnership with operating departments and their managers? How many steps do you think only operating managers should do?

Answering these questions is important. There is no one "right" answer; rather, the answers may vary depending on who is to be recruited, what are to be his or her work responsibilities, and how much support for the newly hired worker from HR and from operating management is essential from the start.

WHAT SHOULD MANAGERS DO IN RECRUITING AND SELECTING TALENTED PEOPLE FOR THE ORGANIZATION?

Some people believe that operating managers, not HR, should shoulder most of the responsibility for recruiting, selecting, and onboarding employees. (And I can already see you shaking your head and saying "I don't have time for that!" Remember that jugglers can do more than one thing at a time and do them well!)

Consider the case to be made for your devoting more time and effort to recruiting. First, recruiting is not an isolated effort. It is part of your job. HR can help, but it is your job. Second, you have high stakes in what happens in recruitment. The kind of people attracted to apply and chosen to work will influence how well you can get results for your department. It also affects how many people you may have who can be considered promotable. Third, recruiting is part of the job of managing. If you do not see people during the recruiting and selection process, then you do not know whose skills were ignored and whose commanded attention. Simply stated, you have too big of a stake in recruiting to just dump it on HR.

Also remember that the professional circles in which you move may be wonderful avenues for recruiting. As you do work for the company, you are ideally positioned to note people who could be recruited for positions ranging from entry level to senior level. You should not do just one thing at a time. You should always be thinking about what talented people could be recruited and what they could do in your organization. You are already a recruiter whether you know it or not. The question is whether you are taking full advantage of your position to leverage it toward recruiting advantages.

> **BILL'S TIP – HIRING**
> If you are in a big hurry to get a new hire on board, there is a danger that you will select someone who is only adequate. Don't fall for that temptation. Hang tough and go for those who are productive *and* promotable.

The war for talent is not going to be won by those too shy or too unwilling to fight.

APPLICATION QUESTIONS

1. Make a list of the steps in your organization to recruit and select people. Indicate how much involvement each operating manager has in each step. Then indicate how much or what kind of involvement you believe each operating manager should have in each step. Explain why you believe as you do.

2. Recruiting talented people may have to be done differently from recruiting just anyone (a "warm body"). List some innovative approaches to *recruitment* that may be especially helpful for your

organization. As just one example, we know that people tend to have friends like themselves. How often does your organization ask high potentials in the organization to recommend applicants?

3. What might be the danger of relying on the opinion of just one person—such as a manager—to make a selection decision?

5

Training and Developing Talented People

Training is any short-term effort designed to equip individuals with the knowledge, skills, and attitudes they need to get acceptable, or even outstanding, work results. Of course, training can occur on the job, near the job, or off the job. It can be conducted in many media—most notably onsite training conducted in a classroom or online training conducted via the Web.

Development is any long-term effort designed to equip individuals with the results of work experience necessary to prepare them for future, perhaps higher level, responsibility. Development is the most important element in preparing talented people for realizing their potential, and about 90 percent of all development occurs on the job. One organization—the Center for Creative Leadership in Greensville, SC, identified at least 88 ways to develop workers on the job in its 1989 publication, *Eighty-Eight Assignments for Development in Place,* by M. Lombardo and R. Eichinger. While you may be tempted to send people outside the organization or department for training to prepare them for the future, the reality is that the most important development occurs on the job. It is under your direct, immediate control. The challenge is how to manage it.

To determine how people develop, answer the following questions:

- With whom do they come in contact with? (supervisors, customers, coworkers, and subordinates)
- What do they do? (type of work and type of assignments)
- When are they tasked to perform? (that is, how much time pressure they face)
- Where do they work? (How much exposure have they had to different parts of the company? Different geographical locations? Different groups or types of customers, suppliers, or distributors?)
- Why are they asked to work? (How much have workers been tasked to start up something new? Shut down something old? Automate a previously manual system? Turn around a failing operation? Deal with dramatically different groups or cultures or locations?)
- How are they asked to work? (How much exposure have they had to doing the work by themselves? Guiding a team? Working as part of a team? Working across teams? Working across conflicted groups to achieve a common goal?)
- How much or how many resources have they been given to do the work? (How much exposure have they had to projects where they are understaffed, underfunded, and otherwise faced with insufficient resources to obtain the desired results?)

Development does not occur in isolation from work; rather, it should be interwoven with work. You are the decision-maker guiding this. To do that, you need to determine development gaps for individuals and plan work experiences that will build the competencies they need to perform successfully in the future, perhaps at a higher level of responsibility. This requires creativity—and the juggling ability of a master.

WHAT THE HR DEPARTMENT SHOULD DO TO TRAIN AND DEVELOP TALENTED PEOPLE FOR THE ORGANIZATION

As in recruiting and selecting workers, you should not believe that HR will do all the work in training and developing your workers. HR can help, but HR professionals do not see the workers every day. You *do*—or, at least *should*—see them every day.

WHAT MANAGERS SHOULD DO TO TRAIN AND DEVELOP TALENTED PEOPLE FOR THE ORGANIZATION

Most of the responsibility for training and developing talented people in an organization rests with the immediate supervisor. It is not a responsibility that can be completely delegated. You shape people based, in part, on what experiences you choose to give them.

Training is rarely, if ever, sufficient to prepare people for promotion. However, good training can narrow performance gaps between what people know, do, and feel and what they must know, do, or feel to perform their current jobs successfully. The difference between what people can do and what they must do to perform acceptably is called a *performance gap.*

It should be emphasized that training should be considered the solution of last resort rather than the solution of first resort. Why? Simply because good training is very expensive. If people have done the job right once, they do not need training. Instead, other action is needed. Additional training will not solve most problems. Only 10 percent of all organizational problems can be solved by training.

Of course, newly hired workers usually *do* need training. They often don't know who depends on the results of their work, what to do, when to do it, how to do it, why it is worth doing, or how to measure results to ensure it was done right. Good training should clarify the answers to all of these questions. And, even workers who are not being groomed for promotion need continuing training to keep skills current. The simple fact is that in today's business environment, it is necessary to run to stay in the same place. Training is not an employee benefit or a luxury to cut when times are bad. Rather, training is essential to ensure continued productivity, so it is especially important when times are bad.

Should you do the training yourself? Well, of course, that would be the ideal. There is nothing that focuses workers' minds so much as having their immediate supervisors carry out the training. In that case, it is impossible for workers to avoid taking responsibility for their actions.

But, in practical terms, you may not be able to do all the training yourself. You may have too much to do—and too little time—as it is. But you still need a good system for training and receiving feedback on how your workers are performing in training. And you need surrogates on whom you can rely to train people properly. You must hold those surrogates accountable for what they do, how they do it, and what results they get from the workers. Of course, the workers themselves should also be held accountable for participating actively in the training.

HOW MANAGERS SHOULD TRAIN AND DEVELOP WORKERS

Consider: What should you do to train workers? Develop workers? This section focuses on answering these questions.

Training

As the previous section indicated, you may not necessarily carry out the process of training everyone, but you should establish a *system* to do so. This system should meet certain clear requirements. It should (1) be focused on making people as productive as possible as quickly as possible; (2) be focused on the work the person is to do (although onboarding may include elements to make the person feel welcome, such as a peer mentoring effort); (3) be conducted primarily on the job and while the person is expected to achieve certain milestones in work results; and (4) be organized, clear, and hold both the learner and trainer accountable to the manager.

Job-focused training can be conducted on the job. On-the-job training, sometimes called OJT, has consistently been shown to have the best return on investment in training. However, there is a difference between unplanned and planned OJT. Effective OJT is planned in a systematic way, based on what new hires need to know to do their work. Ineffective OJT is unplanned and involves "following people around" or "sitting next to someone" as its primary method.

To carry out planned OJT, you need to determine what new hires need to know, when they need to know it, and how they should be trained. A good starting place is an approach like the DACUM method. DACUM is an acronym that stands for "developing a curriculum." While many Web sites describe the approach in detail, the basic idea is to pull together a group of experienced workers and have them describe what they do every day. Then, that information can be verified and turned into a checklist to guide OJT. See a sample job map in Exhibit 5–1 and a sample of a checklist format in Exhibit 5–2.

You may also have to partner with HR or other departments to meet government training requirements (such as Occupational Safety and Health Administration [OSHA]-required training) or company-required training on diversity, sexual harassment avoidance, or other issues. Additionally, training that is required for groups of workers, such as new hires, may be cost-effectively managed by the HR department by designing and delivering the training as a service to managers.

At the same time, workers may be trained on how to be better learners. They should be told, perhaps as early as new hire orientation, that they are expected to take the initiative in learning what they need to be productive on the job. Workers must be told that they are not to be passive learners who sit around and wait for someone to tell them what to do. Rather, they should take the initiative to ask questions, watch more experienced performers do their jobs, and try to imitate people identified as good role models.

Developing

Your real juggling challenge is to develop talented people every day. That has to occur as part of getting out the daily work. It is a very important responsibility if you are to manage talent successfully.

Again, at about this point, you are telling yourself that it just isn't possible. You already have a plate that is so full the food is falling off. You may feel that you just don't have time to develop your workers for the future.

But that may simply mean that you don't know how to do it. The trick is to juggle. (Even better is to build talent management into your daily work program so that you absorb it along with your other responsibilities.) In this way, you accomplish your daily work goals while simultaneously providing coaching, encouragement, and challenges that will develop the talented people on your staff.

The first step is awareness of the need to develop talent every day. Instead of dumping that responsibility on HR or blaming senior managers for giving you the extra responsibility, your challenge is to realize that this is a vital task if you are to cultivate talented people for the future of your division, department, or organization.

Exhibit 5-1. DACUM Research Chart for Middle Manager

DACUM Panel

Tom Barley
Managing Partner
Thomas Barley & Associates

Joe Frash
Vice President of Education
Associated Builders &
    Contractors, Inc.

Angelo J. Frole
President
A.J. Consulting

Charles T. Saunders, Jr.
Project Manager/Audit Services
American Electric Power Co.

Gary Vigorito
Director
Public Utilities Commission

Thomas Weaver
President
ISH Contract Services, Inc.

DACUM Facilitators

Robert E. Norton
CETE/OSU

Christine Overtoom
OSU Consultant

Sponsored by

COLUMBUS STATE
Community
College

Produced by

CENTER ON EDUCATION
AND TRAINING FOR EMPLOYMENT
COLLEGE OF EDUCATION
THE OHIO STATE UNIVERSITY
1900 Kenny Road • Columbus, Ohio 43210-1090

Used by permission of Ohio State University

(continued)

Exhibit 5-1. Continued

DACUM Research Chart for Middle Manager

Duties

Tasks →

Duty					
A Develop Work Unit Operations Plan	A-1 Review business plan for alignment with operations plan		A-2 Identify target customers & expectations	A-3 Develop work unit mission statement	A-4 Identify SWOT
	A-11 Identify tactics to support strategies	A-12 Develop deployment process for operations plan			
B Implement Work Unit Operations Plan	B-1 Announce operations plan to stakeholders	B-2 Solicit feedback from stakeholders	B-3 Review operations plan based on feedback	B-4 Solicit stakeholder support	B-5 Establish schedule for operations plan implementation
C Manage Work Unit Human Resources	C-1 Administer company policies & procedures	C-2 Develop work unit policies & procedures	C-3 Administer work unit policies & procedures	C-4 Provide work unit job analysis	C-5 Create work unit job descriptions/ job specifications
D Manage Work Unit Fiscal/Physical Resources	D-1 Develop work unit budget (C&O)	D-2 Secure work unit budget (C&O)	D-3 Administer approved work unit budget	D-4 Safeguard assets according to company procedures	
E Maintain Work Unit Stakeholder Relationships	E-1 Identify work unit stakeholders	E-2 Identify work unit stakeholder expectations	E-3 Negotiate stakeholder expectations	E-4 Resolve stakeholder concerns	E-5 Develop plans to meet stakeholder expectations
F Maintain Work Unit Business Operations	F-1 Manage work unit personnel work activity	F-2 Manage work unit work flow systems	F-3 Manage work unit production activities (e.g., special projects)		F-4 Monitor work unit facilities operations
	F-12 Evaluate business trends & information for work unit action		F-13 Enforce safety & health procedures		
G Evaluate Work Unit Business Performance	G-1 Establish work unit performance measurement procedures		G-2 Assess work unit performance (actual vs. best practices)		G-3 Assess work unit performance (actual vs. goals)
H Pursue Professional Development	H-1 Identify gaps in skills & knowledge	H-2 Develop a professional growth plan	H-3 Participate in community activities	H-4 Read professional literature	H-5 Utilize professional listserves

SWOT =   Strengths, Weaknesses, Opportunity, Threat
C & O =   Capital & Operating

A-5 Identify work unit goals & objectives	A-6 Identify expectations of work unit	A-7 Identify critical success & quality control factors	A-8 Create business strategies for work unit	A-9 Identify required resources (e.g., physical, fiscal, plant)		A-10 Align organizational structure with operations plan
B-6 Establish logistics for operation plan implementation	B-7 Align work unit resources with operations plan					
C-6 Select work unit personnel	C-7 Assign work unit employee performance objectives	C-8 Administer compensation plan	C-9 Assess work unit employee training needs	C-10 Provide work unit employee training	C-12 Conduct work unit employee performance reviews	
D-5 Maintain work unit physical resources						
E-6 Implement plan to meet stakeholder expectations		E-7 Revise plan according to stakeholder feedback				
F-5 Maintain productivity standards	F-6 Monitor work unit process control standards	F-7 Verify adherence to quality control standards	F-9 Align work unit market operations trends with plant		F-10 Manage work unit business risks	F-11 Maintain company productivity plan
G-4 Solicit feedback from customers & stakeholders to improve work unit performance		G-5 Develop action plan to improve work unit performance	G-6 Implement work unit performance improvement work unit plan			
H-6 Participate in continuing education	H-7 Attend to personal health	H-8 Participate in professional organizations & conferences		H-9 Complete increasingly more difficult/challenging work unit projects		

(continued)

Exhibit 5-1. Continued

General Knowledge and Skills	Worker Behaviors	
Leadership skills*	Manage business climate	Diplomatic
Mentoring skills*	for honesty, integrity	Initiative
Coaching skills*	and ethical behavior	Entrepreneurial
Organizing skills	Ethical	Deals with
Presentation skills	Enthusiasm	ambiguity
Delegation skills	Professional	Open-minded
Negotiation skills	Sense of humor	Dependable
Communication skills (oral, written, listening,	Intuitive	Integrity
body language)	Tenacity	Endurance
Business Law, (Labor, Contract, Government)	Positive mental attitude	Optimistic
General business knowledge	Fair	Common sense
Directing	Responsible	Assertive
Analytical skills	Honest	Perseverance
Time management skills	Flexible	Patient
Diversity skills	Empathetic	Team player
Facilities management	Self-motivated	Consistent
General math skills (statistics)		
Computer skills		
Financial management		
Project management		
Global awareness		
Decision making skills		
Technical proficiency		
Interpersonal skills		
Planning		
Interviewing		
Facilitation skills		

Tools, Equipment, Supplies, and Materials	Future Trends and Concerns
Planning tool (Palm, Daytimer)	e-Commerce
Copy/fax machine	Continuing pressure on corporate profits
Computer w/Internet	Changes in workforce
Calculator	Demographics
Printer	Inadequate training programs
Software	Trend toward longer career & fewer career changes
Professional library	Greater emphasis on work-life balance
Car	Downsizing
VCR/DVD player	Accountability for unethical behavior
Conferencing equipment	Geo-political trends
	Mergers & acquisitions
	Greater requirements for qualified workforce
	Global-Geo-Economic trends
	Changing technology
	Political unrest
	Increased diversity
	Increased stress on individuals

* Leadership, mentoring, and coaching skills are critical throughout all duties and tasks
  of the middle manager's job.

Exhibit 5-2. A Sample Checklist Format

List of Work Activities, Duties, or Responsibilities	Has the Worker Been Trained on the Work Activities, Duties, or Activities?				
1	Yes √	No √	Trainer Initials	Trainee Initials	Trainer Comments
2					
3					
4					
5					
6					
7					
8					
9					
10					

The second step is to realize that the challenge is not to work harder—that is, do more things—but to work smarter—that is, get more impact from everything you do. Developing others need not be something new. It may simply be about doing what you have always done, but with a new focus on getting results today while *also* grooming people for tomorrow.

The third step is to figure out how to do that development. Most of the time I think this is the real reason why managers don't develop talent. They simply don't know how to juggle it along with their daily work. They assume that it must be something new. As a result, they dismiss it out of hand because they don't see how they have time for it.

Realize that development occurs in many ways.

Begin by thinking of development as focused on the person. You have to pay attention to each of your key reports. What are the strengths and weaknesses of each person? What do they do especially well on their jobs now? What could they improve? What knowledge, skills, attitudes, or other essential competencies or qualifications do they lack before they will be promotable? If your organization has a competency model for each level, compare the person to the behaviors linked to each competency for the next higher level of responsibility. Then, focus development on building their ability to perform important behaviors they must master.

You may also need to devise a written development plan for each person. Some people call that an Individual Development Plan (IDP). Perhaps the HR department has already given you such a form. But even if HR has not given you such a form, realize that an IDP usually consists of several key parts:

- What is the development gap between what people can do at present and what they must be able to do to perform at a higher level of responsibility in the future?
- What specific, measurable objectives can be established to narrow that development gap?
- How (that is, through what means) can those objectives be met? Remember that people are developed by whom they come in contact with, what they do, when they are tasked to perform, where they work, why they are asked to work, how they are asked to work, and how much or how many resources they are given to do the work.
- When (over what time span) should those objectives be met?
- How will results be compared to objectives? In short, how are the impacts of the learning experiences compared to the development gap?

See the sample Individual Development Plan (IDP) appearing in Exhibit 5–3. Use it if it is helpful to you.

Exhibit 5-3. A Sample Individual Development Plan

An Individual Development Planning Form	
Name of the Person to Be Developed	Supervisor's Name
Today's Date For the Period	Purpose of Development
Part I. What are the Development Needs?	
Part II. How Will the Person Be Developed?	
Part III. How Will the Success of the Development Efforts Be Evaluated?	
Supervisor's Signature and Date	Individual to Be Developed Signature and Date

Do you have to use an IDP? Of course not. Use whatever works for you. Even a napkin can work if done right. But make sure it works. Just do it.

If you do have an IDP and have it completed as an action plan, you must act on it. What actions does the IDP call for from you as manager? What time, money, and effort must you personally devote to helping implement the plan and thereby narrow developmental gaps for the individual you have targeted? What could you do every day to help contribute to the talented individual's development? You may wish to make a list of things you could do every day to:

- Encourage the person to develop himself or herself.
- Help the talented person gain a realistic sense of his or her own abilities.
- Expose the person to other people, places, work assignments, or time-sensitive challenges that would build their competencies and thereby help make them promotable.
- Sponsor these people with higher level managers.
- Reassure talented people, even when they make mistakes or feel crushed by challenges.

At the same time, do not focus purely on weaknesses. Remember the strengths of these talented people. Be sure to:

- Compliment people on what they have done well.
- Say "thank you" for work well done.
- Say "please" when you ask for something difficult.
- Connect people with strengths to those who need to work on those areas so that they can learn from each other.
- Tell people very specifically what you believe they are really good at—and take time to brainstorm with them how they could leverage their strengths to their own (and the organization's) advantage.

How much time would it really take to do some of these things every day with each of your key reports and with their reports? Try to overcome the tendency to come up with excuses for why you can't do it. Focus instead on simple, practical ways that you *can* do it.

Use the worksheet appearing in Exhibit 5–4 to brainstorm a list of ways that you could work on developing talented people every day.

Exhibit 5-4. A Worksheet for Brainstorming How to Develop Workers Every Day

Directions: Use this worksheet to help you structure your thinking. List as many ways as you can think of that you could use every day to develop your workers. Consider, for instance, whom they could learn from, what kind of work assignments would develop them, where they could be sent that would develop them, what they could learn from time-sensitive assignments, and anything that you believe might be important to reinforce or develop with individuals. List as many things as you can think of. You may wish to consult other managers and see how many ideas they can come up with. Add more space as necessary.

What could you do to help individuals develop on a daily basis?		What would the activity teach people? What kind of competency would it build or what skill or knowledge would it develop?
1		
2		
3		
4		
5		

APPLICATION QUESTIONS

1. Think back to a manager who influenced the kind of manager you are. That influence could have been simply creating a model of behavior for you to follow. What did that person *say* or *do* to encourage you? How did that person act when you disappointed him or her? Now consider how often you do the same things with your own employees. Make a list of action steps you could take to be more encouraging and supportive.

2. Training occurs inside and outside planned learning experiences, such as classroom-based leadership development programs, online programs, or off-site experiences at universities. Describe what role you now play—and what role you should play—in encouraging people to apply on the job what they have learned in training. For instance, do you (and should you) meet with people before they are sent to off-the-job training to clarify what you hope they will learn? Do you (and should you) follow up with people after they have returned from off-the-job training to establish new accountabilities for what you expect them to do on the job based on what they learned?

3. Research shows that on-the-job training has the highest return on investment. But on-the-job training can be planned around learner needs or it can be unplanned and haphazard. How do you plan for the on-the-job training of new hires? For those who have been given new responsibilities? For those who are promoted? How do you—and how should you—improve the nature of on-the-job training given to your workers?

4. People are developed through whom they work with or for, what they do, what time pressures they are given to meet and how they handle those pressures, where they have worked (both in the organization and across different cultures), what specific challenges they have been given (such as setting up a new operation, closing down an old operation, turning around a failing department or location), and how they are expected to achieve results. List the workers who report to you and then make a list of all the development experiences they should have that would equip them to be more promotable. Then plan for how you could give them those experiences.

6

Encouraging Career Planning and Offering Career Counseling

Career planning is the process of deciding what people want to do in the future. A subset of *life planning,* which includes aspects of one's personal life, it centers on selecting an occupation or profession, seeking a job, gaining more responsibility, and potentially changing occupations or fields of interest. At present, workers between the ages of 18 and 38 change careers, jobs, or employers an average of 10 times.

A 2006 study of 7,000 employers in Australia found that 51 percent offer planned career programs to their employees (Hudson, 2006). These employers believe it is important to do that to retain talent, focus their development efforts, show employees what's in it for them, and build loyalty to the firm. A 2003 study of 100 companies, conducted by Hewitt, found that those companies that use a planned process to help workers advance in their careers tended to be high-performing organizations as measured by total returns to shareholders.

Career counseling is the process of helping other people reflect on their careers. It is a planned approach to helping a worker reflect on his or her competencies and deciding how to use or improve them for the future. Career counselors don't "tell people what to do"; rather, they facilitate an individual's decision-making process by providing information or access to people who can help the person understand what may be required to achieve his or her career goals. While some people do career counseling full time, you can—and should—carry it out as a manager or supervisor. Remember, you have the greatest impact on your workers.

WHAT THE HR DEPARTMENT SHOULD DO TO ENCOURAGE INDIVIDUALS TO TAKE CHARGE OF THEIR CAREERS

HR bears an important part of the responsibility for establishing some of the systems if the organization wants to approach career planning in a systematic way. At this strategic level, HR should help the organization's leaders to:

- Clarify the purpose, measurable goals, and policy to govern the career program.
- Clarify the work done and competencies required now.
- Determine how performance is measured.
- Clarify the work to be done in future and the competencies required if the organization's strategic plan is to be realized.
- Give individuals and/or managers objective ways to assess pro- motability.
- Allow individuals to work with their managers to set career plans, using individual development plans.
- Periodically evaluate the results of the career planning effort.

In additional, HR can establish so-called "career centers" and deliver "career counseling" off the job and away from the manager in case individuals aspire to move to other departments or locations.

HOW MANAGERS CAN ENCOURAGE INDIVIDUALS TO PLAN THEIR CAREERS

You bear an important, and indeed key, responsibility in career planning and counseling. Indeed, you exert great influence over the development of your workers by the example you set and the challenges you give your workers as part of their everyday work. You, as a manager, *do* matter in the aspirations of your workers. You can encourage or discourage their beliefs in themselves and their hopes for the future.

But what specifically should you do? Here are a few practical suggestions.

First, analyze your people collectively and individually. What are their strengths and weaknesses? What does the staff, as a team, do especially well? Poorly? Have you provided feedback on both strengths and weaknesses to them collectively and to each person on the team? Do you follow up on that regularly rather than waiting until the ritual of a once-a-year performance appraisal?

Second, create a vision that becomes the vision of the team and each member. What should the future look like for them individually and collectively? Talk to the team as a group about the future. Also talk *regularly* to each member of the team about short-term and long-term career goals, showing active interest in what each individual wants to do in the future. Listen carefully.

In some cases, you may feel that a person's goals are unrealistic. If so, then ask tough questions. But avoid the temptation to discourage them, since that can be damaging to their egos and accomplish nothing more than make them angry with *you*. Simply point them in the direction of issues that may be barriers to their own progress, ask tough questions about their abilities, and give them ideas about how to overcome those issues.

If talented people are uncertain of themselves—and that sometimes happens—then be encouraging. Give them opportunities to build their self-esteem and self-confidence. Avoid tearing them down, which is really a danger for you if, like most managers, you have been trained to be critical and analytical! A person who genuinely lacks self-confidence needs to be built up! But the most important thing you can do is to be supportive of them.

Do not be threatened if your worker says something like, "I want your job!" In fact, that is a wonderful thing to hear, because it means that they are begging you for help. They do not know what you know because they lack your experience or perspective. They need your help, encouragement, coaching, and mentoring!

Third, create a sense of urgency and help people see where the organization, and the business environment, is going. Emphasize that you can help them develop for the future but taking the initiative is up to them! It is not your job to do everything for them, but you should give them advice on what actions might have the greatest impact on their future.

Fourth, encourage people to establish personal and career action plans. Too many people just float in the water, without swimming in any direction, and expect wonderful things to drift toward them. But people with visions and plans beat those without them every time. The reason is that people with plans know how to prepare to take advantage of future career opportunities and avert possible future career threats.

Fifth, help people implement action plans. Ask what you can do to help. Then carry through and do what you promised.

Sixth, communicate about the plan regularly. Ask members how they feel the team is doing—and what team members could do to improve. Focus not just on work results but on how team members work together and interact, since group interaction does affect results. Ask individuals how they feel they are doing on their personal and career action plans. Make time to talk about it. Encourage people to come talk to you about their plans. And offer *daily* encouragement.

Seventh, encourage people to step back and reflect on their career plans periodically. This is especially important when major changes affect them, such as a merger, a takeover, an acquisition, or some other major, and perhaps surprise, announcement of an organizational change. Take individuals aside and talk to them about what the change could mean for them and their plans. When you do not know the impact, tell them the truth.

HOW THE HR DEPARTMENT CAN HELP WITH CAREER COUNSELING

> **BILL'S TIP – CAREER COUNSELING**
> When you talk to others about their future, be sure to touch on two things: (1) What interests them personally and what they are good at; and (2) What is happening outside the organization in the competitive environment that could affect future opportunities.

The HR department should establish a strategic framework to help individuals acquire information about careers inside and outside the organization. HR should also offer services to individuals that describe what qualifications they might need to be promotable and how they can obtain those qualifications. Finally, HR should provide services off the job and away from the manager to discuss individuals' problems on the job.

HOW MANAGERS CAN HELP INDIVIDUALS WITH CAREER COUNSELING

While career counseling can be conducted by professionals who make it their life's work, almost anyone can play the role of career counselor. Have you ever had occasion to talk to other people about their career

BILL'S TIP – CAREER COUNSELING

Make time for career counseling, but realize that you do not need to be an HR professional or a licensed psychologist to carry out good career counseling. The most important thing is to demonstrate to other people that you care about them. That can be done by a word, a glance, a gesture, and in many other ways. It does not necessarily mean extra work, but it may mean you have to juggle to do more than one thing at a time!

decision-making? For instance, most parents have had some discussion with their children about career goals. Coworkers sometimes talk about their plans for the future. Even friends may discuss their jobs—and their career aspirations—over beers or in casual conversation. If you have had any or all of these experiences, you have had some exposure to career counseling.

Workers look up to their immediate supervisors. They expect them to be knowledgeable. That gives a manager credibility in offering advice about what people should do to prepare for their careers.

Career counseling does not have to be some formal activity. It can be woven into daily conversations and actions. But how?

Here are a few simple things you could do every day to carry out career counseling with your talented workers. Ask them questions like:

- What did you do today to help prepare for your future?
- What is the most important thing you learned today?
- What was the most exciting thing you did today, and why did you find it exciting?
- What did you enjoy most about your work today? What did you enjoy least? Why?
- What is the biggest problem you faced on the job today, and how did you resolve it?

- How did your work today contribute toward helping you achieve future career goals?
- What could you do every day to contribute to achieving your career goals?
- What did you learn about yourself today?
- What was the biggest contribution you made today?
- What could you improve tomorrow at work that would help toward meeting your career goals?

As a manager, you do not need to offer formalized career counseling all the time. But simply showing that you care—and that your door is always open to discuss it—is enormously powerful in developing the talent of your people. And show that you mean it. Don't look at your watch when people ask to talk to you. Make time for it.

Use the worksheet in Exhibit 6–1 to help structure a career planning and counseling session based on the questions above.

APPLICATION QUESTIONS

1. How often have you specifically encouraged your workers to come to see you to discuss their career goals? How could you do that more often and in more welcoming ways? Come up with a list of action steps that you could take more often.
2. Suppose one of your workers comes you for career advice. The first thing he or she says is, "I want your job someday." How would you respond to that? How do you think you *should* respond to that?
3. Imagine that one of your best workers comes to see you for career advice. That worker makes it very clear that he or she never wants to be promoted and merely wants to continue doing the same job. Suppose that you have always (secretly) assumed

Exhibit 6-1. Questions for You to Consider About Your Career

Directions: Consult these questions each day and write out your answers.
Discuss with your immediate supervisor if you wish.

Questions for Consideration		How Would You Answer These Questions?
1	What did you do today to help you prepare for the future?	
2	What is the most important thing you learned today?	
3	What was the most exciting thing you did today, and why did you find it exciting?	
4	What did you enjoy most about your work today? What did you enjoy least? Why?	
5	What is the biggest problem you faced on the job today, and how did you overcome it?	
6	How did your work today contribute toward helping you achieve your future career goals?	
7	What could you do every day to help you contribute to achieving your career goals?	
8	What did you learn about yourself today?	
9	What was the biggest contribution you made today?	
10	What could you improve tomorrow in how you are working toward meeting your career goals on a daily basis?	

that this worker was your own back up and likely successor. How would you handle the situation?

4. You have a worker who is very proficient. She is outstanding on the technical side of the work your department handles, but you have had many complaints about how bad this person is in handling interpersonal situations. Another manager once told you that "she is just terrible with people." She comes to you for advice on how to be considered for promotion. What advice would you give her?

5. You have a worker who performs below average on the job. It is not bad enough to warrant corrective action, but it is noticeably below the standards set by average workers in your area of responsibility. She comes to you, confident that she deserves promotion, and asks for a raise and for a job title that will place her above the other workers. How would you respond to this situation, and why?

7

Performance and Development Coaching

If there is one chapter in this book that is critically important, this is the one. Coaching is a term that is often used in businesses today. But how many managers have received skill-based training on coaching and really know how good coaching can be woven into what they do every day? I suspect very few can point to such an experience. You could get a Harvard MBA and never receive hands-on, skill-based training on coaching. And yet it may be the single most important thing that a manager can do to groom talent for the future.

What is coaching, and why is it important in managing talent? How are the terms performance coaching and development coaching defined? What step-by-step model can guide coaching? This chapter answers these questions.

WHAT IS COACHING, AND WHY IS COACHING IMPORTANT FOR MANAGERS IN MANAGING TALENT?

Coaching is a process that is intended to help people improve their performance. While sometimes associated with sports, it can exist in many spheres. There are life coaches, personal coaches, business coaches, health coaches, sports coaches, dating coaches, and conflict coaches—to name but a few.

In recent years, much attention has been devoted to executive coaches. That is not surprising. Organizations that have not done a proper job of succession planning or talent management make it a practice to promote individuals who are not properly prepared for higher level responsibility. When that happens, the organization's leaders may insist on success with a coach as a condition for individuals to retain these promotions. Rather than make promotions "sink-or-swim" experiences for employees, life preservers in the form of coaches are thrown to employees. If people do not possess sufficient knowledge to do the work, they may need *job content coaches* who have successfully done the work before. If people are perceived to lack essential interpersonal skills, then they may be given *job process coaches* to shadow them and provide instant, private feedback on how to improve interactions with staff members, customers, or others. Many professional associations offer formal certification for coaches and executive coaches.

Why is coaching so important to the manager's role? First, you, as a manager, are best positioned to observe your workers and notice when coaching may be needed. Good managers do that subconsciously, often without realizing that they are coaching. Second, you should be familiar with the expected work results and are in a position to see what workers are doing. Gaps between what workers are doing and what is needed to achieve results may prompt you to comment on what to do, how to do it, when to do it, why it is important to do, and what results are sought—and why. When you intervene to do that, you are offering coaching. Third, development is often inextricably interwoven with coaching. You may comment on how worker activities may relate to preparation for higher level responsibility, as in "I asked you to work on that section of the budget because I wanted you to see how that is done. That is the hardest part of preparing the budget. When I was in your position, nobody showed me how to do it, and I had to struggle when I was promoted to learn how. If you ever sit in my chair, I don't want you to have to go through the pain I had to go through to learn that." That exchange indicates developmental coaching is the reason why the manager asked the worker to do the task. And it reemphasizes to the worker what he or she has done and why it is important for the future.

DEFINING PERFORMANCE COACHING AND DEVELOPMENT COACHING

Performance coaching focuses on helping workers do their present jobs better or faster. You use performance coaching when workers need on-the-spot advice about how to do their jobs. *Development coaching* focuses on helping workers prepare for higher level responsibility. You use development coaching when workers have an opportunity to do something on the job that would prepare them for higher level responsibility, such as being a back up for you when you are away.

> **BILL'S TIP – COACHING**
> To do a good job in coaching, remember that you must have a plan of action (a game plan), link the plan to individual career goals, drill yourself by practicing how to coach, suit how you talk to your listeners, and take steps to congratulate people when they perform well.

Use performance coaching when you believe the worker needs to improve his or her performance. Use development coaching to groom someone for possible future higher level responsibility.

Note that this is not rocket science. Anyone can do it—and you can do it as part of what you do already. This does not necessarily require extra work. It does require that you integrate it with what you do already. So, the trick is to juggle and figure out how to incorporate into your current job additional coaching for improved performance and for developing your most talented people.

A STEP-BY-STEP MODEL TO GUIDE DAILY COACHING

Since coaching can occur all the time, it must be guided by a simple approach—a model—that you can easily remember. The steps for performance coaching are listed in Exhibit 7–1 and described below.

- *Step 1:* Describe what you see the worker doing.
- *Step 2:* Describe what the worker should be doing.
- *Step 3:* Explain why the difference between steps 1 and 2 is important.
- *Step 4:* Offer specific advice on what the worker should do—and demonstrate the right way, if possible.
- *Step 5:* Ask the worker to try it while you observe.
- *Step 6:* Watch the worker do it.
- *Step 7:* Congratulate the worker if he or she does it right; offer feedback for improvement if the worker does not do it right.

Use the worksheet appearing in Exhibit 7–2 to help you plan such coaching.

Exhibit 7-1. The Steps in Performance Coaching

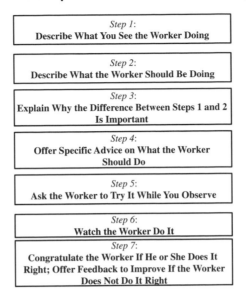

Step 1: **Describe What You See the Worker Doing**

Step 2: **Describe What the Worker Should Be Doing**

Step 3: **Explain Why the Difference Between Steps 1 and 2 Is Important**

Step 4: **Offer Specific Advice on What the Worker Should Do**

Step 5: **Ask the Worker to Try It While You Observe**

Step 6: **Watch the Worker Do It**

Step 7: **Congratulate the Worker If He or She Does It Right; Offer Feedback to Improve If the Worker Does Not Do It Right**

Exhibit 7-2. A Performance Coaching Checksheet

Directions: Use this checksheet to guide a performance coaching experience. Plan your coaching and then follow the steps below when helping workers improve their performances in their present jobs.

Steps in Performance Coaching	Did You Follow These Steps?	
Did you...	Yes √	No √
1 Describe what you saw the worker doing?		
2 Describe what the worker should be doing?		
3 Explain (specifically) why the difference between steps 1 and 2 is important?		
4 Offer *specific* advice on what the worker should do—and demonstrate the right way, if possible?		
5 Ask the worker to try it while you observe?		
6 Watch the worker do it?		
7 Congratulate the worker if he or she did it right; offer feedback to improve if the worker did not do it right?		

Exhibit 7-3. Steps in Development Coaching

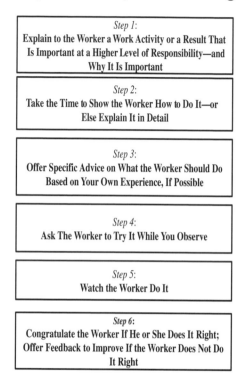

> *Step 1:*
> Explain to the Worker a Work Activity or a Result That Is Important at a Higher Level of Responsibility—and Why It Is Important

> *Step 2:*
> Take the Time to Show the Worker How to Do It—or Else Explain It in Detail

> *Step 3:*
> Offer Specific Advice on What the Worker Should Do Based on Your Own Experience, If Possible

> *Step 4:*
> Ask The Worker to Try It While You Observe

> *Step 5:*
> Watch the Worker Do It

> *Step 6:*
> Congratulate the Worker If He or She Does It Right; Offer Feedback to Improve If the Worker Does Not Do It Right

Development coaching is similar. But its focus is a little different. Use these steps, depicted in Exhibit 7–3 and described below:

- *Step 1:* Explain to the worker an activity or a result that is important at a higher level of responsibility—and why it is important.
- *Step 2:* Take the time to show the worker how to do it—or else explain it in detail. Use an example from the work, if possible.
- *Step 3:* Offer specific advice on what the worker should do based on your own experience, if possible.
- *Step 4:* Ask the worker to try it while you observe.
- *Step 5:* Watch the worker do it.
- *Step 6:* Congratulate the worker if he or she does it right; offer feedback to improve if the worker does not do it right.

Use the worksheet appearing in Exhibit 7–4 to help you plan such coaching.

It is worth noting that even if you just offer words of encouragement, you are playing a critical role as a coach. Encouragement can take many forms. You can congratulate the worker on hard work, express appreciation for the worker's efforts, or remark on how skilled the worker

BILL'S TIP – COACHING

Be willing to say "it's my fault . . ." when your workers make mistakes, even if it is not your fault. Good coaches have high self-confidence and are willing to take the blame so that the focus can be on improving the worker rather than placing blame.

Exhibit 7-4. A Development Coaching Checksheet

Directions: Use this checksheet to guide a development coaching experience. Plan your coaching and then follow the steps below when helping workers develop themselves for future responsibility.

Steps in Development Coaching		Did You Follow These Steps?	
Did you...		Yes √	No √
1	Explain to the worker a work activity or a result that is important at a higher level of responsibility—and why it is important?		
2	Take the time to show the worker how to do it—or else explain it in detail and use an example from the work, if possible?		
3	Offer specific advice on what the worker should do based on your own experience, if possible?		
4	Ask the worker to try it while you observe?		
5	Watch the worker do it?		
6	Congratulate the worker if he or she does it right; offer feedback to improve if the worker does not do it right?		

did something. Often a few words will have a more powerful impact than most supervisors realize. It is worth taking time—and making time—just to do that.

APPLICATION QUESTIONS

1. One way to learn is to watch other people who are good at something and then simply try to imitate what they did and how they did it. This approach is called social learning theory, a fancy name for what essentially means "monkey see, monkey do." We can learn by watching and imitating others. Think of someone you have known or observed who was especially good at coaching. Think how that person performed. Make a list of what the person said, the body language the person used, and then try to imitate that with one of your employees. If you can't think of anyone to emulate, then ask around and find someone other people think is good at this. Make an effort to watch them in action.

2. Coaching can be done in a series of steps, as the chapter indicates. Alternatively, a manager may use only one or several steps in a longer coaching model. Think about what one or more steps you could take to coach your workers every day. Make a list of action steps. (Those steps do not need to include all the steps in the coaching models described in the chapter.)

3. You can learn from bad examples as well as from good ones. Think of someone you know whom you would say is the worst at coaching that you have ever seen. What are or were the bad habits of that person? (Example: a worker makes a mistake and the manager, instead of criticizing the person in private, does so publicly.)

4. Imagine that you are given the chore of developing a training program for managers on coaching. How would you teach them to do it?

8

Appraising Workers and Providing Daily Feedback

Say *performance appraisal,* and most managers will make a face as if they just bit into a lemon or gulped sour milk. It is not a popular topic Many, perhaps most, managers feel that today's performance management systems are a just a waste of their valuable time, a conspiracy by HR departments to make their lives more miserable by saddling them with unnecessary and burdensome paperwork. The time they have to spend on appraising performance and filling out performance appraisal forms, they feel, could be put to better use in dealing with more important matters. If managers are asked why they feel this way, they will usually comment on how bad the forms are.

But, of course, performance appraisal means more than just a form. Performance management is not a system driven by a form. Rather, it occurs on a daily basis through the feedback that managers—and customers and workers' peers—provide. An annual performance appraisal should never be a surprise because the continuing feedback given to workers provides ample indications in advance of what they have been doing well, what they should improve, and how they should improve. Performance appraisal actually coincides with the continuous supervision that managers should demonstrate with the people reporting to them.

PERFORMANCE MANAGEMENT

Terms can be confusing so it can be helpful to define terms first.

Defining Performance Appraisal and Performance Management

Performance appraisal is a process of evaluating how well workers are reaching their goals. While job descriptions set forth what workers do, a performance appraisal evaluates how well workers did it over a given time. In most cases, the appraisal focuses on quality, quantity, cost, time, and customer service issues associated with employee performance.

Performance management implies more than appraisal. It includes an entire cycle that begins with planning the work and the results to be achieved, monitoring employee behaviors and results achieved, developing employees' abilities, evaluating behaviors demonstrated and results achieved, and rewarding results. Unlike performance appraisal, which may suggest after-the-fact performance review, performance management includes an entire cycle of jointly and collaboratively planning the work to be done, assessing it as it is carried out, and documenting results achieved and the means by which those results were achieved. Therefore, a performance management system is more robust than a typical performance appraisal approach that emphasizes documentation.

Reasons for Performance Appraisals and Performance Management

Performance appraisals are carried out to: (1) give feedback to employees on how well they are performing their work; (2) pinpoint training needs; (3) document results; (4) justify pay raises or other rewards; (5) offer an opportunity for communication between worker and the organization's management; (6) validate the way the organization chooses people for various jobs or work; and (7) provide a basis for other employment decisions such as discipline, wage increases, and promotions.

Recent thinking about performance management emphasizes developing key performance indicators (KPIs). These focus on the results needed most from each job and devote special attention to measuring it according to the organization's strategy. This strategy is expressed through a balanced scorecard that stresses achievement on more than just profit; it places equal weight on achievement in finances, customer service, work processes, and learning and growth.

HOW ARE PERFORMANCE APPRAISALS AND PERFORMANCE MANAGEMENT RELATED TO TALENT MANAGEMENT?

It is worth spending a moment to comment on how performance appraisals and performance management relate to talent management.

One fundamental principle of talent management is that individuals should not be promoted to higher level responsibility solely because they are doing a good job where they are. After all, work at a higher level calls for new competencies. Consequently, success at a lower level does not guarantee success at a higher level of responsibility.

But there is a corollary to that. And that is that individuals should not be promoted if they are failing or doing poorly in their current jobs at their existing level of responsibility. To promote those who are failing sends the wrong signal to employees. It destroys the credibility of the promotion system and will prompt other workers who are performing well to cry foul.

Either after-the-fact performance appraisal or more holistic performance management that plans, monitors, and reviews performance is thus critical to talent management. The reason is that performance appraisal or performance management protects the integrity of the talent management system. Either one provides a means by which to document performance coaching and reward performance at the individual level of responsibility. Without it, organizations would be at a loss as to who is really doing his or her current job well. That alone could raise questions about the fairness—and the quality—of promotion decisions.

HOW IS PERFORMANCE APPRAISAL CARRIED OUT ON A DAILY BASIS?

You may associate performance appraisal with an annual ritual that includes forms to be completed. But, in reality, performance appraisal is a process that goes on all the time, whether you know it or not. Your smile or frown to an employee is a form of performance appraisal. How you talk and how you look at your workers are forms of appraisal. In short, you have many ways to appraise employees. You do so all the time in every interaction with every worker. How you appraise also shapes the behavior of your workers.

The ultimate test of an annual performance appraisal is that it contains no surprises. The workers already know what you think of their performance because the annual appraisal is just a summary of the feedback they have been getting from you on a regular basis. *The point worth emphasizing here is that you should be providing an appraisal to each worker on a regular basis and should pay close attention to the signals you are sending to workers about what you think of them and their work performance!*

This does not mean you have to conduct a formal meeting with workers each day. But you *can* give workers some kind of feedback all the time to indicate how they are doing. That can be done through methods as simple as a short e-mail or a "hello, good job today" in the hallway or cafeteria. A smile can do it. You can walk through the work area at the end of the day and give a short, impromptu performance review to each worker. That does not have to take long. But the immediacy of the feedback is powerful. It also shows you *care*.

Just avoid the tendency to pounce on people when they are not doing well or when they just made a mistake, particularly if you ignore them when they have been performing adequately—or exceptionally. That is not good management. And it will lead to dissatisfied, demoralized workers who do not like or respect their immediate supervisor. It can, and does, prompt absenteeism and turnover.

HOW IS PERFORMANCE MANAGEMENT OR APPRAISAL CARRIED OUT MORE FORMALLY ON AN ANNUAL BASIS?

Remember that the key, traditional difference between performance management and performance appraisal is where they start. Performance management is holistic and thus involves facilitating the planning, monitoring, and reviewing of worker performance. But performance appraisal only occurs after the performance is demonstrated and results are obtained.

Performance management begins by clarifying the relationship between the organization's measurable goals and objectives, the department's measurable goals and objectives, and the worker's job and expected work results. The balanced scorecard is the governing idea. According to Harvard professors Kaplan and Norton, who first described the balanced scorecard, the goal is to regard organizational performance on a broader range of criteria than simple profitability. They suggested that four key criteria should be used instead: financial, customer, internal business process, and learning and growth measures. These criteria should be based on the organizational leaders' vision and strategy.

Each worker's job, the theory goes, relates to organizational strategy and measurable balanced score card criteria in specific ways. These most important measures are called key performance indicators (KPIs). Many organizations today measure workers' performance in two ways: what measurable results they achieve compared to their KPIs and how they achieve those results by demonstrating behaviors associated with good or outstanding performance. Hence, KPIs tie to organizational and work needs, and behaviors tie to the competencies required for success at a specific level of performance, such as supervisor or manager.

Each step of the performance management cycle is really needed to create a robust system for examining performance. Results must be planned; results must be monitored; and, results must be evaluated. At the same time, the behavior used to achieve results must also be planned, monitored, and evaluated.

BILL'S TIP – APPRAISING PERFORMANCE

You have a responsibility to make employer expectations clear and measurable. Clarify the targets you expect and the minimum work standards that must be achieved. Don't leave that to chance, and don't pretend you are too busy. Workers can't perform if they don't know the expectations!

As a manager, you are key to the whole process. You must sit down with workers at the beginning of a review cycle — such as at the start of the year—and plan what results they should achieve and how they should achieve them. A key focus should be the KPIs for the worker's job. At periodic intervals—such as quarterly—the individual's progress toward the KPIs should be formally reviewed. At the end of the cycle, the individual's achievements should be evaluated.

While you may complain about a performance appraisal or performance management form, the reality is that the meetings to plan, monitor, and review performance are the most important part of the process. It is not the form but rather *how you use it* that matters. And the meeting is where you come face to face with the person. Some research shows that if the meeting is mishandled, it can actually lead to reduced performance and productivity because the individual will be demoralized!

How is a good interview conducted? First, whether the interview is intended to create performance goals, monitor and review recent performance, or evaluate results over the review period, you will need to plan for it. Decide whether it will be designed to "tell and sell," "tell and listen," or "problem solve." In a "tell-and-sell" interview, you have already decided what results you want; in a "tell-and-listen" interview, you bring your own ideas about the individual's performance to the meeting, share them, and then listen with an open mind to what the worker has to say; in a "problem-solving" interview, you share some concerns you have about the worker's performance and then set out with the worker to try to solve the problems that may be creating barriers to success.

> **BILL'S TIP – APPRAISAL**
> Feedback is essential in performance appraisal. Research reveals that one-sided feedback, such as managers provide when giving one-sided reviews, tend to be rejected as biased. Workers regard feedback as more valid when it comes from sources most familiar with their daily work. In short, 360-degree feedback can be particularly effective, as can feedback given directly by customers without managers in the middle.

Begin interviews by setting people at ease. Ask about their feelings and how things are going. Use appropriate body language to show that you are listening actively. (That means hold the phone calls and don't look at your watch! Pay attention to the person!).

Manage the interview by explaining what it is for and what is to be accomplished. If you wish, you may ask workers to do a draft of the key performance indicators and the performance plan for the year. Then read them, correct them, and take some time to share information about the organization's and the department's strategic objectives. You may even share information about your own KPIs and those of the department. Talk about challenges faced by the business and department. Then work with individuals to finalize their documents. Ask questions throughout the process to involve the workers and avoid appearing to make all decisions.

The same basic approach can also be used in monitoring interviews and in the final annual review.

Should all interviews be the same? Probably not. High potentials often come to performance review meetings with a sense of dread. One reason is that their personal standards may be higher than their immediate supervisor's standards. They always feel that they are not doing as well as they could be doing. The simplest words of criticism from the supervisor may be devastating to them. Hence, special care may need to be taken, depending on the type of person. A good approach with them is for you to begin by asking what is worrying them or how they think they are doing and why they think that.

Of course, the reverse situation can also be true. Some high potentials are supremely self-confident and even arrogant. Words of criticism bounce off them like bullets off Superman. They just don't hear them. For them, specific examples must be provided—and more than one—before you will begin to get through to them. One powerful approach is to put it in writing ahead of time and give them the write up in the meeting to review. Spell out what they are doing, what they should be doing, what the difference is, why the difference is important, how long you will give them to improve, and what will happen if they don't improve. That approach is perhaps the best way to deal with supremely self-confident people who may not otherwise hear criticism. At the end, ask what they commit to do to change. See if it matches what you have asked for. If not, make sure they understand what the consequences will be for failing to improve.

WHAT IS MEANT BY "PROVIDING DAILY FEEDBACK?"

Feedback is the process of providing information to people about how well they have performed and are performing. Good feedback does not, and should not, have to wait for the formal performance management system. Instead, it should be interwoven with supervision. Indeed, being a good manager means you are good at giving and receiving feedback.

Providing continuous feedback means that you let people know where they stand on their performances every day. You can do that in a number of ways.

Good feedback shares the same characteristics as good goals. They are S.M.A.R.T.

S.M.A.R.T feedback is

Specific

Measurable

Attainable

Realistic

Timely

What does that mean?

Specific means that it is very clear. It answers all the key journalistic questions of who, what, when, where, why, and how. *Measurable* means that the feedback can be quantified.

> **BILL'S TIP – GIVING FEEDBACK**
>
> Giving good feedback can be hard work. Be clear, positive, specific, behaviorally focused, and descriptive. If possible, explain the impact on others of the workers' behavior. Show that you believe what you say by using "I" rather than "others are saying."

Attainable means that the feedback leaves the door open for improvement—and individuals see how they can achieve results. *Realistic* means that the feedback is tied to something that people are willing, and able, to achieve. And *timely* means that good feedback occurs as soon as possible after the event that prompted it.

WHAT STEP-BY-STEP MODEL CAN GUIDE THE DAILY PROCESS OF PROVIDING FEEDBACK?

What should be the steps in giving feedback?

Note that you should avoid giving *destructive feedback*—that is, criticism that is given in public, criticism that cannot be acted on, and criticism that is insulting and destroys self-esteem and self-confidence. Remember to praise in public, but criticize in private. Talk in terms of how to do the work better, not in terms of what's wrong. And never attack the person ("boy, are you stupid!"), but focus on the behavior or results desired.

To give good, *constructive feedback,* see the diagram in Exhibit 8–1, which is based on the following steps:

- Mention the goal to be achieved, the results desired, and/or the behavior that is desirable.
- Clarify what people are doing, being specific but not insulting.
- Describe what people should be doing; be specific.
- Clarify how to narrow the gap as specifically as you can.
- Reemphasize the importance of the task, the results to be achieved, and the behavior.
- Explain how their performances make you feel.
- Ask for an explanation from workers, if they wish to provide it.
- Listen to what workers have to say and offer suggestions.
- Demonstrate the right way, if time permits.

- Confirm that workers know what to do and how to do it.
- Summarize the action that workers have committed to take.
- Express your thanks.

Exhibit 8-1. The Steps in Giving Effective Feedback

Step 1: **Mention the Goal to Be Achieved, the Results Desired, and/or the Behavior That Is Desirable**

Step 2: **Clarify What the Person Is Doing, Being Specific But Not Insulting**

Step 3: **Describe What the Person Should Be Doing, Being Specific**

Step 4: **Clarify How to Narrow the Gap in as Specific Terms as You Can Possibly Provide**

Step 5: **Reemphasize the Importance of the Task, the Results to Be Achieved, or the Behavior**

Step 6: **Explain How the Person's Performance Makes You Feel**

Step 7: **Ask for an Explanation from the Worker, If He or She Wishes to Provide It**

Step 8: **Listen to What the Worker Has to Say and Offer Suggestions**

Step 9: **Demonstrate the Right Way, If Time Permits**

Step 10: **Confirm That the Worker Knows What to Do and How to Do It**

Step 11: **Summarize the Action That the Worker Has Committed to Take**

Step 12: **Express Your Thanks**

It may also be useful to train workers how to ask for feedback from you or from others. They should follow these basic steps in requesting feedback:

- Explain what has been done.
- Clarify how you feel about it.
- Ask for help in looking it over.
- Explain the specific feedback desired.
- State when the feedback is desired and in what form.
- Express thanks and appreciation.

As manager, you should remember that some workers want or need almost constant feedback; others don't want or need it that often. Use your judgment in deciding when to give feedback. Considering the person—and perhaps his or her generation. Some observers of the contemporary business scene believe that people from different generations have different opinions about feedback.

The four generations in the workforce at present include *traditionalists* (born between 1922 and 1943), *Baby Boomers* (born between 1943 and 1960), *Generation Xers* (born between 1960 and 1980), and *millenials* (born between 1980 and 2000). Although there is always the danger of stereotyping, in general, the traditionalists would rather get as little feedback as possible; Baby Boomers want it held to a minimum and documented thoroughly; Gen Xers want it periodically; and millenials would like it almost constantly. You may wish to ask your workers how often they want feedback—good or bad—and in what form they would prefer it.

Use the daily feedback form appearing in Exhibit 8–2 to help guide your ability to give effective feedback.

Exhibit 8-2. A Worksheet Based on Steps in Giving Effective Daily Feedback

Directions: Use this worksheet to guide you in giving effective daily feedback. For each step appearing in the left column below, indicate in the center column whether you have taken that step when you have occasion to give someone feedback.Then, in the right column, take notes about what you should say–or how you could improve what you did in the situation.

Steps in Giving Effective Daily Feedback	Did You Follow Those Steps?		What Should You Say or How Could You Improve? (*Notes*)
Did you (or do you plan to):	Yes √	No √	
1 Mention the goal to be achieved, the results desired, and/or the behavior that is desirable			
2 Clarify what the person is doing, being specific but not insulting			
3 Describe what the person should be doing, being specific			
4 Clarify how to narrow the gap in as specific terms as you can possibly provide			
5 Reemphasize the importance of the task, the results to be achieved, or the behavior			
6 Explain how the person's performance makes you feel			
7 Ask for an explanation from the worker, if he or she wishes to provide it			
8 Listen to what the worker has to say and offer suggestions			

(*continued*)

Exhibit 8-2. Continued

Steps in Giving Effective Daily Feedback	Did You Follow Those Steps?		What Should You Say or How Could You Improve? (*Notes*)
Did you (or do you plan to):	Yes √	No √	
9 Demonstrate the right way, if time permits			
10 Confirm that the worker knows what to do and how to do it			
11 Summarize the action that the worker has committed to take			
12 Express your thanks			

APPLICATION QUESTIONS

1. How do you prepare plans for your workers' responsibilities over the coming year? Describe the process, and then explain how you might take advantage of that opportunity to also plan for their development.

2. How do you give workers daily feedback in your area of responsibility? Are you a "seagull" manager (to paraphrase Ken Blanchard, author of the best-selling book, *The One Minute Manager*) who leaves people alone when they are doing well but only gives them feedback by "zapping them" when they do something wrong?

3. How do you think you could *improve* the way you give workers daily performance feedback, complimenting them when they perform well and giving them coaching when they could improve?

4. Most of the time, organizational leaders think of performance appraisal or performance management as focused on individu-

als. But might there be ways that you could give regular feedback to the whole group (work unit, department, or division) on their performance? If so, what might that look like, and how could use that process to improve the way talent is managed in the organization?

9

Managing High Potentials, High Performers, and High Professionals

Managers sometimes believe they should treat all their workers alike. To do otherwise, as every experienced manager knows, is to beg for complaints that the manager is playing favorites. That can lead to uncomfortable questions about why the manager is doing so.

But not all people are equally talented. If people were equally talented, then everyone would possess the musical abilities of a Mozart, the mathematical abilities of an Einstein, and the artistic abilities of a Picasso. We all know those people were exceptions because they were extraordinarily talented. Few people possess such extraordinary abilities in specific areas. And that means some people may need to be managed differently from those who are not so gifted.

What is a high potential, a high performer, and a high professional? And why are these people important to talent management programs? What should managers do on a regular basis to manage high potentials, high performers, and high professionals? By addressing these important questions, you will learn how to manage these so-called *high flyers,* that is, people with unique talents.

WHAT IS A HIGH POTENTIAL (HIPO), AND WHY ARE HIGH POTENTIALS IMPORTANT TO TALENT MANAGEMENT PROGRAMS?

The term *High Potential,* sometimes abbreviated as *HiPo,* is a specialized term that has several meanings. Organizational leaders should make explicit what they mean by the term. And you, as a manager, should follow that definition once it is clarified.

Of course, there is the old joke that the opposite of a HiPo is a PoPo—someone who is *pissed off and passed over.*

More seriously, though, the possible definitions of HiPos apply to those who:

- Are doing at least acceptable work where they are, but are also promotable because they already meet the competency demands of the next level.
- Are doing at least acceptable work where they are, but are capable of promotion to two or more levels higher on the organization chart within five years based on objective assessment, such as an assessment center or a 360-degree assessment.
- Are capable of being promoted to CEO at some future time. (Note: In some nations and cultures, it can be predicted with some certainty who will be in the pool of possible future CEOs based on family, political or personal affiliations, and schools attended. For example, members of a royal family do not start at the bottom and work their way up, but are, instead, immediately eligible for senior positions based on their status).
- Are well matched to the organizational leaders' definition of an HiPo, which may be specialized. Indeed, an organization's leaders may define in advance what they regard to be essential for designation as a HiPo. People who measure up to those criteria are thus regarded as HiPos.

Why is the definition of a HiPo important?

Consider that organizational leaders have only so much time and money to devote to development. Like any investment, investing in people should be well advised and well considered. Investing in the development of some people is more likely to pay off than investing equally in everyone.

For this reason, then, identifying the HiPos makes it possible for organizational leaders to invest training and development funds wisely by focusing on those who are most likely to benefit the organization in the future. In short, knowing who the HiPos are makes it easier to target development efforts. It also shows organizational leaders how strong the organization's bench strength is, so that they know when external recruitment is needed and when qualified internal candidates exist to fill current and future vacancies.

WHAT IS A HIGH PERFORMER (HIPER), AND WHY ARE HIGH PERFORMERS IMPORTANT TO TALENT MANAGEMENT PROGRAMS?

A *High Performer,* sometimes called a *HiPer,* is another specialized term with several meanings. Organizational leaders should make explicit what they mean by the term. And you, as a manager, should follow that definition once it is clarified.

Of course, there is the old, corny joke that HiPers are Hyper—that is, hyperactive. Sometimes, that is true. They may be very energetic people who strive for results unceasingly.

More seriously, though, the possible definitions of HiPer apply to those who:

• Consistently outperform the average, measurable performance level of workers in their job category, or

- Are the most outstanding performer(s), based on objectively assessed measures of productivity, in their job categories.

Another way to define a HiPer is anyone who has maintained a sterling reputation with senior leaders in the organization. Note that the first definition depends on objectively measurable performance; the second depends on perceptions of competence that stem from political support within the organization. It is important not to confuse the two. People can be outstanding but get little or no recognition; people can be merely average but get outstanding recognition. The question is how much objectivity leaders want and demand.

HiPers are not the same as HiPos. They do their jobs exceedingly well—and may, in fact, be the single best performers in their job categories. But they may not want a promotion or they may not be appropriate for promotion because they lack the necessary competencies or qualifications to move up the ladder.

WHAT IS A HIGH PROFESSIONAL (HIPRO), AND WHY ARE HIGH PROFESSIONALS IMPORTANT TO TALENT MANAGEMENT PROGRAMS?

A *High Professional,* sometimes called a *HiPro,* is another specialized term with several meanings. Organizational leaders should make explicit what they mean by the term. And you, as a manager, should follow that definition once it is clarified.

The possible definitions of HiPro are those who are the in-house experts on:

- Specific problems, challenges, or issues that confront the organization (here the focus is on their ability to solve specific problems).
- Unique, important organizational work processes (here the focus is on their special knowledge about how to weave through com-

plicated, and even byzantine, work processes to get results, despite obstacles that may be thrown up).

- Specific technical or functional competencies of the organization (here the focus is on their exceptional ability in *only one area* of specialized work).
- The history of the organization and how the organization overcame past (here the focus is on the HiPro as a repository of *institutional memory*, meaning what has happened in the organization's history).

Many organizations do not know who their HiPros are. They are not given the same special care and feeding as HiPos (who may be in grooming for promotion) or HiPers (who are rewarded with better-than-average raises on an annual basis). They are indeed sometimes the unsung heroes of the organization.

But identifying the HiPros is critical in an emergency. When a unidentified aircraft flies over any sovereign nation, the government scrambles jets to chase it and bring it down. When an organization faces a crisis, the managers should scramble the HiPros to get fast, effective results. The HiPros are the primary repository of wisdom on work processes and organizational history. Their knowledge of special issues is higher than that of anyone else—including HiPos.

HiPros are not the same as HiPos or HiPers. They do their jobs at least adequately. But they are the *most knowledgeable* about what to do, when to do it, and how to do it.

WHAT MANAGERS SHOULD DO ON A DAILY BASIS IN MANAGING HIGH POTENTIALS, HIGH PERFORMERS, AND HIGH PROFESSIONALS

Since the first philosophy of management was published by Frederick W. Taylor in 1915, much of the literature on management has emanated from the United States. These writings have been written as if everyone should be managed the same. Management textbooks do not distinguish among different approaches that may be appropriate for managing different kinds of workers. And, indeed, managers often worry when they treat one worker differently from the others—even when justification exists.

The bane of any manager is to be accused of favoritism. Worse yet is to be accused of discrimination that leads some people to receive more favorable advancement opportunities or rewards than others because of matters unrelated to performance, such as race, religion, sex, age, disabilities, or sexual orientation.

But in recent years, a new idea has emerged that is worth considering for its implications for management practice. As part of the increasing interest in talent management to deal with the problems of an aging global workforce, large employers have begun to classify their employees according to current job performance and the potential for advancement. Worth emphasizing is the assumption that success at one level (and on one's current job) does not guarantee success at higher levels (and possible advancement opportunities). The reason is that each level of management—from supervisor

---

BILL'S TIP – MOTIVATING HIPOS

Establish a work climate that motivates HiPos by:

1. Making the work challenging.
2. Setting realistic goals.
3. Showing appreciation for work well done.
4. Showing enthusiasm for good ideas, approaches, and results.
5. Taking steps to determine what people want. Don't assume everyone wants the same thing. Then, do whatever you can to give people what they want when they warrant it by their results.

BILL'S TIP – DEMOTIVATING HIPOS

Managers may not be able to motivate others, since motivation comes from within. But they may be able to demotivate HiPos. Here are the common ways. Be sure to avoid the following:

1. Giving people too much work to do. ("The reward for good work is not a pay raise or promotion but more and harder work!")
2. Watching everything they do; say nothing about what they do well, but pounce fiercely on what they do wrong.
3. Being miserly in praise. ("Damn with faint praise.")
4. Ignoring bad performers but riding the good ones when they make mistakes.
5. Encouraging people to come to you for permission on everything, thereby encouraging people to take no responsibility.

to manager to executive—requires different knowledge, skills, attitudes, and other characteristics for success.

As noted in previous chapters, it is also well known that individuals do differ dramatically in their abilities to get results. In fact, the research suggests that the most productive workers in any job category may be *as much as 20 times more productive* than their equally qualified but less productive or less talented peers. The most productive workers may require special "care and feeding" from their immediate supervisors. If not managed well, they could leave the organization—and their departure could represent the equivalent of losing as many as 20 people! That hurts in today's highly competitive, downsized workplace.

Think of it another way. Would you pay attention to an 800-pound gorilla or a 20-foot-tall person? If you say yes, then just remember that your most productive worker may actually outweigh that gorilla many times. If the average American weighs about 150 pounds—and that is being kind in an age of obesity—then your best worker could be just like a 3,000-pound gorilla! Alternatively, if the average American is about 6 feet tall, the best worker could be the equivalent of 120 feet tall!

While the management literature is relatively sparse on applying different management approaches to different employee groups, the literature on a related topic has been the focus of some attention in education. Educators have long practiced *ability tracking* in schools. While actual practices do not always live up to the theory, much has been learned about the unusual issues associated with teaching gifted students. *Gifted students* are, of course, those with recognized talents who transcend their peers.

Now consider this question: *Could some of the same approaches applicable to teaching gifted children apply to managing high-flyer workers?* It is a topic that fires the imagination. It may mean that one-size-fits-all management strategies are not appropriate—and perhaps never were. Workers who regularly and consistently outperform their peers should be managed differently. That idea alone may mean that every management textbook currently in print requires revision. It goes beyond simplistic situational leadership notions that apparently base different management approaches primarily on workers' experience levels.

Consider what has been written about the characteristics that teachers of gifted children should possess. William Heath wrote a treatise in 1997 that pulled together the existing research evidence on what is known about teaching gifted children. Citing previous research from varied sources, he summarized the characteristics needed by teachers of gifted children. According to him, such teachers must exhibit:

- A thorough understanding of the subject they are teaching.
- Self-confidence and a strong sense of self.
- A good sense of humor.
- Excellent organizational skills.

- Openness and flexibility in their approaches to teaching.
- Better-than-average self-esteem.
- Strong communication skills.
- A high level of intelligence.
- An ability to delight in the learning process itself.
- Curiosity and a willingness to experiment with dramatically new, and often previously untried, approaches.
- A very high energy level.
- An understanding of the gifted (though not necessarily be gifted themselves).
- Friendliness.
- An ability to establish high standards and a near preoccupation with excellence bordering on perfectionism.
- A willingness to be an advocate with higher-ups on behalf of learners.
- Enthusiasm for what they do.

Two additional issues are worthy of special note. The first is that the most common source of complaint among the parents of gifted students centers on what their childrens' teachers *do*—or *fail to do*. Second is that research on gifted children has found that the teacher cannot go it alone; the school must also establish a climate that encourages gifted children to realize their potential.

Take a moment to rate yourself on these important competencies for managing HiPos. Use the tool appearing in Exhibit 9-1.

The research summarized above may contain profound implications for the managers of HiPos, HiPers, and HiPros. Although still a theory, it could mean that managers of the most talented workers should possess characteristics similar to those identified for the teachers of gifted children. In short, high-flyer workers may need managers who demonstrate the special skills necessary for supervising such highly productive, talented (and sometimes temperamental or, alternatively, self-esteem-challenged) workers. And, while all managers should probably possess most of the same char-

Exhibit 9-1. Assessing the Unique Competencies Required of Managers of High-Performing and High-Potential Workers

Individuals require different management approaches to get best results. Not all individuals are the same. Managers who work with high-performing (HiPer) workers and who work with high-potential (HiPo) workers may have to possess specialized competencies to be most effective. A HiPer is, of course, defined as an employee who consistently outperforms others in the same work group or job category. A HiPo is defined as an employee who has the potential to be promoted 2 or more levels in 5 years or less. Use this worksheet to assess your own competencies as a manager to demonstrate these special competencies.

Think of the special competencies required of managers who oversee HiPers and HiPos. Some of them are listed in the left column. For each competency listed in the left column below, rate how well you feel you demonstrate these competencies in the center column. Use this scale: **0 = I do not feel this competency is applicable; 1 = I need to improve my ability to demonstrate this competency to a large extent; 2 = I need to improve my ability to demonstrate this competency to some extent; 3 = I feel that I do not need very much development on demonstrating this competency; 4 = I feel that I demonstrate this competency very well**. Then, in the right column, make notes about how you believe you could improve your ability to apply these competencies.

Special Competencies Managers Need to Develop HiPers and HiPos	How Well Do You Feel That You Can Demonstrate This Competency					Notes on How You Could Improve Your Ability to Apply These Competencies
	0	1	2	3	4	
1 A thorough understanding of the function you are managing	0	1	2	3	4	
2 Self-confidence and a strong sense of self	0	1	2	3	4	
3 A good sense of humor	0	1	2	3	4	
4 Excellent organizational skills	0	1	2	3	4	

5	Openness and flexibility in their approaches to teaching	**0**	**1**	**2**	**3**	**4**	
6	Better-than-average self-esteem and self-confidence	**0**	**1**	**2**	**3**	**4**	
7	Strong communication skills	**0**	**1**	**2**	**3**	**4**	
8	A high level of intelligence	**0**	**1**	**2**	**3**	**4**	
9	An ability to delight in the work process itself	**0**	**1**	**2**	**3**	**4**	
10	Curiosity, flexibility, and a willingness to experiment with dramatically new, and often previously untried, approaches	**0**	**1**	**2**	**3**	**4**	
11	A very high energy level	**0**	**1**	**2**	**3**	**4**	
12	An understanding of what it feels like to be a HiPer or HiPo	**0**	**1**	**2**	**3**	**4**	
13	Friendliness	**0**	**1**	**2**	**3**	**4**	
14	An ability to establish high standards	**0**	**1**	**2**	**3**	**4**	
15	A near preoccupation with excellence that borders on perfectionism	**0**	**1**	**2**	**3**	**4**	
16	A willingness to be an advocate with higher ups on behalf of HiPers or HiPos	**0**	**1**	**2**	**3**	**4**	

(*continued*)

Exhibit 9-1. Continued

Special Competencies Managers Need to Develop HiPers and HiPos		How Well Do You Feel That You Can Demonstrate This Competency					Notes on How You Could Improve Your Ability to Apply These Competencies
		0	1	2	3	4	
17	Enthusiasm for what you do	0	1	2	3	4	
18	Other competencies that they feel are essential. (List them)	0	1	2	3	4	

acteristics, what may set effective from ineffective managers apart is their *ability to demonstrate these characteristics to an exceptional degree and on a daily basis.* And employers also have an obligation, just as schools do, to establish a climate that encourages talented workers to exercise and cultivate skills that generate first-rate productivity.

What complicates matters is that there are at least three kinds of talented workers—HiPos, HiPers, and HiPros. There could be other special groups as well—such as HiEs (who demonstrate exceptional ethics when confronted with temptations) and HiVs (who represent the highest embodiments of the values most prized by the organization). It could be that specialized management skills are required by supervisors who oversee each special and highly productive or talented, employee group. These special abilities could be assessed and perhaps developed among managers.

Use the Worksheet appearing in Exhibit 9-2 to solicit information from other managers in your organization about the special

(*text continued on page 142*)

Exhibit 9-2. Identifying the Unique Competencies Required of Managers of High-Performing and High-Potential Workers

Not all individuals are the same. Managers who work with high-productive (HiPer) workers and who work with high-potential (HiPo) workers may have to possess specialized competencies to be most effective. A HiPer is, of course, defined as an employee who consistently outperforms others in the same work group or job category. A HiPo is defined as an employee who has the potential to be promoted 2 or more levels in 5 years or less. Your help is needed to identify the most important competencies that are essential for those managers who oversee HiPers and HiPos.

Moment of Truth Activity #1

Directions: Think of a time when you encountered your most difficult challenge in managing a high-performing or high-potential worker. Then answer the questions appearing below. There are no "right" or "wrong" answers. This activity should be completed anonymously. Write on the back of the sheet or add paper as needed.

1. What was the situation? (Describe it in the space below. Tell when it happened, who was involved [job titles only], what it was, and why it was so difficult.)

2. What did you do to handle the situation?

3. What happened as a result of what you did? What were the consequences of your actions?

4. If you encountered the same situation again, how would you handle it? Would you handle it exactly the same as you did, or would you handle it another way? (Explain your answer.)

(*continued*)

Exhibit 9-2. Continued

Moment of Truth Activity #2

Directions: Think of the most common challenge you face as a manager who oversees high-performing or high-potential workers. Then answer the questions appearing below. There are no "right" or "wrong" answers. This activity should be completed anonymously. Write on the back of the sheet or add paper as needed.

1. What is the situation? (Describe it in the space below. Tell when or how often it happens, who is usually involved [job titles only], what it is, and why it is so difficult.)

2. What do you do to handle the situation?

3. What happens as a result of what you do? What are the typical consequences of your actions?

4. How would you train a new manager to handle the situation described above? Explain why you would train the new manager as you advise.

Training Method   **Explanation of Approach**

Moment of Truth Activity #3

Directions: Think of the most common problem or area for improvement you see with managers who oversee high-performing or high-potential workers. Then answer the questions appearing below. There are no "right" or "wrong" answers. This activity should be completed anonymously. Write on the back of the sheet or add paper as needed.

1. What is the problem? (Describe it in the space below. Tell when or how often it happens, who is usually involved [job titles only], what it is, and why it is so difficult.)

2. What do you think is the cause of the problem?

3. What do you think should be done to solve the problem or avoid the problem?

issues they have encountered in managing HiPos, HiPers, and HiPros and reach some conclusions about what special competencies managers may need to cope with these challenges.

APPLICATION QUESTIONS

1. How do you manage your high potentials? Do you treat them differently from the way you treat fully successful (average) workers? If so, what specifically is different? Do you believe this difference is correct, or should everyone be treated similarly?

2. Compare the list of competencies in dealing with highly gifted students to those you use in managing high potentials. What competencies might your organization need to add, subtract, or modify? In which of these competencies do you already feel successful on a daily basis? In which competencies do you feel you could use improvement? List some ways in which you could demonstrate those competencies with your high potentials every day.

3. Imagine that you ran across a person in a social setting whom you believe would be an outstanding prospect for your organization. Suppose further that this person appears to match up well to the profile of high potentials in your organization. What would you say to this person that might convince him or her to apply for a job in your organization? What special appeals might be necessary for a high potential that would be different from the appeal you would make to a less outstanding candidate?

4. What have you noticed about other managers in your organization regarding the way they treat high potentials? Do you see any patterns or similarities? Are those good practices or not, and why do you think so?

10

Transferring Knowledge and Professional Contacts

More is needed in talent management than simply attracting, developing, and keeping gifted people. You, as a manager, are also responsibile for ensuring that experienced workers transfer the knowledge they have gained to the next generation or to their successors. Managers must also ensure that successors know some of the people who contributed to previous successes.

KNOWLEDGE TRANSFER DEFINED

Knowledge transfer is the process of transferring specialized knowledge from one person or group to others. It is sometimes associated with *technical succession planning,* which focuses on transferring experiential wisdom rather than preparing people for promotion. Consider that when experienced workers retire or otherwise leave an organization, they take their experiences and their institutional memory with them. In some cases, that knowledge is proprietary to the business and may be "business critical." For instance, if experienced engineers who have worked for a cell phone company retire,

143

they may take with them their knowledge about the transition from the previous to the present generation of cell phone. If experienced medical researchers retire, they may take with them information acquired over decades about avenues for research to cure a disease. The employer may replace an engineer or a research scientist with a new hire, but they cannot easily replace the knowledge those people gained from years of experience. That knowledge should be transferreed.

TIPS TO GUIDE INFORMAL KNOWLEDGE TRANSFER

Think about what you have done to encourage the transfer of specialized knowledge in your organization. Consider:

- How much documentation exists in your department, division, or work unit about work methods and procedures?
- How much documentation exists in your department, division, or work unit about work processes, methods, tools, and techniques used by employees who possess specialized skills and bear specialized responsibilities?
- How often does your department, division, or work unit plan for retiring employees to mentor replacements before they leave the organization?
- How often are successors permitted to "shadow" a departing worker with specialized knowledge?
- How often does your organization hire or place on contract workers who possess hard-to-replace knowledge?
- How often does your organization encourage videotaping or tape recording of special meetings or other events of importance so that they may be viewed by future workers?
- What special communication approaches, if any, does your organization use to encourage transfer of knowledge?

Use the Worksheet appearing in Exhibit 10–1 to organize your thinking about answering these questions.

Exhibit 10-1. A Worksheet to Organize Your Thinking About Transferring Special Knowledge

Directions: Use this worksheet to do some brainstorming about what you and/or your organization is currently doing to transfer specialized knowledge of value to your organization. For each question in the left column, answer the question in the right column.

Questions	Your Answers
1 How much documentation exists in your department, division, or work unit about work methods and procedures?	
2 How much documentation exists in your department, division, or work unit about work processes, methods, tools and techniques used by employees who possess special skills and bear special responsibilities?	
3 How often does your department, division or work unit plan for retiring employees to mentor replacements before they leave the organization?	
4 How often are successors permitted to "shadow" a departing worker with special knowledge?	
5 How often does your organization hire or place on contract workers who possess special knowledge?	
6 How often does your organization encourage videotaping or tape recording of special meetings or other events of importance so that they may be viewed by future workers?	
7 What special communication approaches, if any, does your organization use to encourage transfer of knowledge?	

TWELVE PRACTICAL STRATEGIES CAN BE USED TO TRANSFER KNOWLEDGE

Strategy 1: Job-Shadowing Programs

A *job-shadowing program* is one approach to transferring knowledge from one person or group to another. A less-experienced performer is paired up with a veteran, who is asked to share knowledge (and perhaps hands-on practice) in dealing with the most difficult situations he or she has faced on the job.

Strategy 2: Communities of Practice

A *community of practice* is a group that comes together to share information about a common problem, issue, or topic. Such communities may meet in person or online. It is a way by which to store and transmit knowledge from one person (or a group) to another.

Strategy 3: Process Documentation

Popular as a result of ISO and the quality movement, *process documentation* involves preparing flowcharts showing how work is performed. It may include special variations in what performers should do or how they should do it based on special circumstances. Clear process documentation, which may include flowcharts or procedure manuals, can be helpful in storing and transferring knowledge from a more-experienced to a less-experienced person.

Strategy 4: Critical Incident Interviews or Questionnaires

First described in the 1950s, this method takes its name from tapping the lessons of experience. A *critical incident* is a difficult (critical) situation (incident). By documenting the lessons learned by the organization's most experienced performers, the organization can capture the fruits of that experience. Of course, by documenting such "difficult cases"—and how they were handled—the organization is also laying the foundation for the development of a manual or automated expert system. Critical incidents provide an excellent foundation for training. An example of a questionnaire designed to capture critical incidents appears in Exhibit 10–2.

Strategy 5: Expert Systems

An *expert system,* usually automated, is organized around problems and how to troubleshoot them. A simple example is the "context-sensitive help" on most word processing programs. (If you should ever call the help desk of a major computer company, the person on the other end of the phone is probably equipped with an expert system.)

Exhibit 10-2. A Critical Incident Questionnaire

Directions: Think about your work experience, and answer the following questions.

1. Think back to a time when you faced the most difficult challenge in your job in this organization. What happened? Describe it in some detail, telling what happened step by step.

2. Who was involved? (*Give job titles, but no names.*)

3. When did this occur?

4. What did you do in the situation, and what were the consequences of your performance?

5. What made the situation so difficult?

6. If you faced this situation again, how would you handle it? Would you change what you did in the original situation? If so, why? If not, why?

Common or difficult problems are logged into the system. Advice about troubleshooting and solving those problems is also provided in the system. This approach, while requiring more technological sophistication, places information at the fingertips of even the least experienced performers, giving them the ability to perform like a pro.

Strategy 6: Electronic Performance Support Systems (EPSS)

Perhaps most sophisticated of all methods for storing and transferring knowledge is an *electronic performance support system* (EPSS). An EPSS combines artificial intelligence, an expert system, real-time e-learning methods, and a computer-based referencing system. As users encounter a problem, they can access all organizational policies and procedures through the referencing system, gain advice based on experience from the expert system, and even learn in real time using the training component.

Strategy 7: Job Aids

A *job aid* is anything that helps people perform in real time. A checklist is a job aid. So is a sign. Knowledge can be stored in the job aid and accessed through low-tech methods by performers when the need arises.

Strategy 8: Storyboards

A *storyboard* is literally a group of pictures that tell a story. Think of a series of pictures placed on a wall or a poster that is intended to show how someone should perform in a specific situation, and you get the idea. For instance, if you were trying to show someone how to perform the Heimlich maneuver (an approach to helping someone who is choking), you could storyboard it. The same technique can be applied to other procedures to provide a graphic representation of what to do and how to do it. Thus, storyboards can be used in storing and transferring knowledge. If HiPros provide information for a storyboard, they may in fact be documenting their specialized knowledge.

Strategy 9: Mentoring Programs

A *mentor* is an experienced performer; a *mentee* is a less-experienced one. Rarely is a mentor a supervisor, since effective mentors should usually have no selfish interest in the development of another person. Successful people have usually had one or more mentors in their careers, and mentors offer advice on what to do, how to do it, and why it is worth doing in a situation. Such programs can, of course, facilitate knowledge transfer. It can be particularly effective if HiPros are paired with less-experienced people.

Strategy 10: Storytelling

Most wisdom in organizations is passed on through storytelling. A *story* is a description of what happened in a particular situation. Most people have heard many stories about their organizations. If you hear "what really happened" in a promotion, demotion, termination, or transfer, you are hearing a story. Storytelling is less structured than critical incidents but can serve the same ends. It can be a most effective way of transmitting wisdom from one person to another.

Strategy 11: Information Exchanges

Have you ever attended a career fair? If you have, you have seen one form of information exchange. The same basic approach can be turned to information exchanges. When this strategy is used, veteran performers sit at booths (or at tables) and dispense wisdom to the less-experienced performers who visit them.

Strategy 12: Best Practice Studies or Meetings

Too often we assume that best practices occur outside our organizations. But it is possible that the organization has its own existing best practices. These can be shared in meetings.

Other Approaches

There are, of course, other ways to store and/or transfer knowledge than the strategies listed above. One way to capture the lessons of experience is for the organization's decision makers to do better than they have historically done in tapping their retiree base. Individuals with valuable knowledge can be placed on retainer to provide one-on-one phone guidance—or even online or video-conferenced advice—to less-experienced workers as they face problems. Managing the retiree base of the organization may prove to be an important trend of the future.

A STEP-BY-STEP MODEL TO GUIDE KNOWLEDGE TRANSFER

Technical succession planning is not carried out in the same way as managerial succession planning for the simple reason that the focus of attention is different. Managerial succession is about finding and developing the "right people" to place in the "right positions" and in the "right locations" at the "right times" to achieve the "right (because strategically important) objectives." The emphasis is really on *who (people)*. Existing roadmaps for managerial succession planning center attention on clarifying what characteristics (competencies) people will need in the future to perform effectively and how to select or develop people to achieve those strategic objectives.

The three biggest challenges facing decision-makers in managerial succession are : (1) avoiding temptations to clone current job incumbents when future conditions may require different skills; (2) erroneously assuming that successful performance at one layer of the organization's hierarchy automatically guarantees success at higher levels; and (3) ensuring accountability of individuals and their organizational superiors for developing talent and not just handling daily work or managing sudden crises.

In contrast, technical succession planning is about isolating, distilling, and transmitting the "right information" to people at the "right times" to ensure the continuity of operations and provide a foundation for future improvements. The emphasis is really on *what*—exclusively the implicit and explicit experiences of running a process and/or operation. The biggest challenge in technical succession planning is the *knowledge transfer problem,* referring to the difficulties of transmitting the fruits of experience to successors. Those setting out to address technical succession planning must isolate relevant knowledge, distill it, preserve it, and find practical ways to transmit it in useful forms to those needing it when they need it and in forms they can use. In short, how do you know what is important, and how do you sidestep concerns from the people who possess that knowledge that capturing it will not be used against them to replace them or eliminate the need for them?

To conduct technical succession planning, consider following this roadmap:

- *Make the commitment:* Decide that there is a need to identify and capture specialized knowledge and institutional memory before the people who possess that knowledge are lost to the organization through retirement, disability, or death.
- *Clarify **what** work processes are key to the organization's mission.* Map key work processes that are essential to achieving the organization's mission. Clarify what results are desired and how they are achieved.
- *Clarify **who** possesses specialized knowledge about these work processes gained from experience.* Examine the work force assigned to each work process to identify individuals who possess, through experience and performance, the most valuable knowledge about the work. Who are the in-house experts on each critical work process, and how do we know they are experts?
- *Clarify **who** the organization may be at risk of losing through retirement or other loss.* Assess eligibility for retirement of those who possess specialized knowledge or experience.
- *Clarify **how** these work processes are performed by those possessing specialized knowledge gained through experience.* Engage in a

planned approach to tapping institutional memory and institutional wisdom. Use planned or unplanned approaches. Examples of planned approaches may include the critical incident method (in which experienced performers are asked to tell stories about the challenges of the past and how they addressed them), storyboarding (in which specific events are illustrated in flowcharts that isolate the root causes of problems), and DACUM charting (in which experienced performers are asked to build work profiles that describe what they do on a daily basis, how they do it, and what they have learned about performing it based on experience). Examples of unplanned approaches may include mentor programs in which people are asked to share experiences or shadowing programs with less-experienced people assigned to watch more experienced ones.

- *Capture and distill the specialized knowledge about those work processes that are possessed by those with specialized knowledge.* Examine the information collected in step 5 above and analyze it by theme or by symptom of a problem.

- *Consider how to maintain and transmit specialized knowledge and who needs it to ensure the efficient and effective continuity of operations.* Once the institutional memory of the most experienced performers has been tapped, it must be captured. Formal ways to do that may include electronic expert systems (which catalog a problem by symptoms and then provide suggested solutions). Informal ways may include training programs, brown bag lunches to discuss the past, and others.

- *Continuously assess knowledge gaps, evaluate the action strategies taken to address them, and the results achieved.* Assess individuals against the knowledge requirements for the work processes, periodically examine what steps are being taken to preserve and transmit institutional memory, and evaluate what results have been gained from these efforts.

These steps are depicted in the roadmap in Exhibit 10-3.

Exhibit 10-3. Steps in Knowledge Transfer

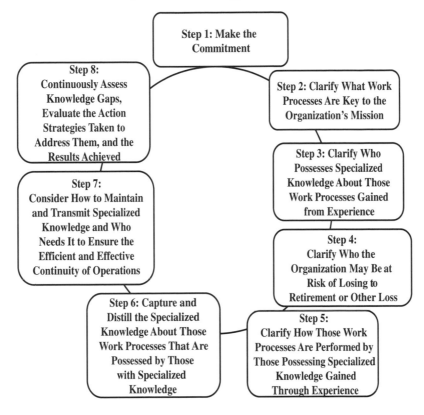

IDENTIFYING AND OVERCOMING BARRIERS TO KNOWLEDGE TRANSFER

Numerous barriers get in the way of knowledge transfer. If you set out to transfer knowledge, you should consider—and plan for—overcoming these barriers. The barriers include the inability of the organization to:

- Focus on what specialized knowledge should be captured.
- Focus on who possesses the specialized knowledge.
- Focus on how to capture the specialized knowledge.

- Focus on how to make specialized knowledge available to those who need it in practical ways.
- Deal with distances or geographical separation of those possessing specialized knowledge and those who need it.
- Deal with differences in language or culture.
- Overcome issues of trust.
- Overcome issues of political conflict among different groups in the organization.
- Recognize differences in the ways different generations access and use information.
- Make it worthwhile for those who possess special knowledge to transfer it.

Use the Worksheet appearing in Exhibit 10–4 to plan how to overcome these barriers.

DEFINING SOCIAL RELATIONSHIP TRANSFER

Succession planning and talent management are issues that are taking center stage as many organizations struggle to prepare for, or weather through, waves of retirements. The aging global work force, coupled with the downsizings engineered by many organizations in a cost-cutting mode some years ago and continuing to this day, has depleted the talent pool of many organizations. While attention has been devoted to management succession planning as a means of building the bench strength of promotable talent and to technical succession planning as a means of preserving institutional memory and knowledge transfer, little attention has been devoted to finding ways to preserve and pass on the social relationships that are so important to business continuity.

Leaders bring more to their jobs than the ability to get the work done. Experienced workers know the institutional memory of

Exhibit 10-4. A Worksheet for Overcoming Barriers to Knowledge Transfer

Directions: Use this worksheet to plan for ways to overcome various barriers to knowledge transfer. For each barrier appearing in the left column below, record your ideas in the right column. There are no "right" or "wrong" answers in any absolute sense, but some ideas may be better than others in the corporate culture of your organization.

Barriers to Knowledge Transfer	What Are Some Ways to Overcome the Barriers to Knowledge Transfer?
1 The inability of the organization to focus on what special knowledge should be captured	
2 The inability of the organization to focus on who possesses the special knowledge	
3 The inability of the organization to focus on how to capture the special knowledge	
4 The inability of the organization to focus on how to make special knowledge available to those who need it in practical ways	
5 The inability of the organization to deal with distances or geographical separation of those possessing special knowledge and those who need it	
6 The inability of the organization to deal with differences in language or culture	
7 The inability of the organization to overcome issues of trust	

(continued)

Exhibit 10-4. Continued

Barriers to Knowledge Transfer	What Are Some Ways to Overcome the Barriers to Knowledge Transfer?
8 The inability of the organization to overcome issues of political conflict among different groups in the organization	
9 The inability of the organization to recognize differences in the ways different generations access and use information	
10 The inability of the organization to make it worthwhile for those who possess special knowledge to transfer it	

their organizations, and the memory of technical workers is particularly important in firms that rely on building on technical knowledge to achieve success. Notable examples include medical researchers and engineers. In both cases, the knowledge that experienced workers take with them when they leave their organizations are valuable and are, in many cases, impossible to replace.

But experienced workers have also established social networks of professional contacts that pay dividends over the years. When these workers retire, these social contacts are lost unless organizations take steps to preserve them by encouraging workers nearing retirement to pass on their contacts and open doors for their successors.

What is social relationship succession planning, and why is it important? What model can guide efforts to conceptualize it? What methods may be used to preserve social contacts as workers prepare to retire? This article addresses these important questions, offering notes for future investigation.

Social relationship succession planning is the process of introducing successors to the professional contacts of individuals who are retiring from their organizations. It is critically important to some work—such as sales, public relations, and government lobbying or government relations. And it involves more work than simply introducing people. To pass on relationships, individuals must arrange for the people to get to know—and, most importantly, *trust*—each other.

Social relationships are important for preserving contacts between an organization and its customers, suppliers, distributors, and other relevant groups on which the organization depends for success. Without making the effort to pass on these relationships, business can be lost—and productivity can suffer.

A *model* is a simplified representation of something that is complex. Models guide conceptualization and are helpful to think-

Exhibit 10-5. A Model of the Social Relationship Succession Planning Process

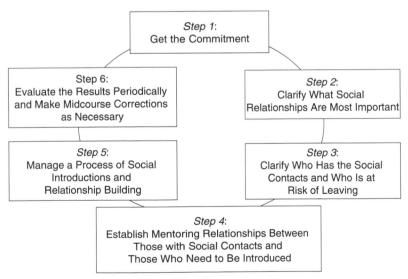

ing about issues. Best practice firms use models to integrate the many components of a succession planning program.

Exhibit 10–5 depicts a model of social relationship succession planning. The steps in the model are described in the sections below.

Step 1: Make the Commitment

The first step is to make the commitment. This involves persuading top managers that it is worthwhile to try to capture the social contacts of key people in the organization. It also involves persuading individuals who have these contacts to identify them.

It is usually not difficult to persuade top managers of the value of identifying important social contacts and helping to pass them on. It makes much sense to do so.

The real challenge is convincing people who have social contacts to identify them and then serve as mentor for others. It must be clear "what is in it for them" to do so. After all, there is value in having social relationships, and by identifying them, those individuals may be giving up a cushion of safety. For that reason, it may be worthwhile to offer incentives to identify and sponsor this process.

Step 2: Clarify *Which* Social Relationships are Most Important

Not all social relationships are important to a business. Only some are. If social relationships make it easier to communicate among customers, suppliers, distributors, and other stakeholders and the business, then it is a value relationship. One place to start is simply to ask workers to suggest possible contacts they have among customers, suppliers, and distributors, and also tell why they are important.

Step 3: Clarify *Who Is at Risk of Leaving*

Once individuals have identified their social contacts, it is then necessary to examine the risk associated with the loss of people who have established these relationships. How likely are people to retire in the short term based on their age? While it is not advisable to ask people whether they plan to retire when they are eligible to do so, it is enough to identify those who qualify for retirement in the future and then take steps to begin passing on their social contacts in preparing for their departure at some unknown time in the future.

Step 4: Establish *Mentoring Relationships* Between Those with Social Contacts and Those Who Need to Be Introduced

Mentoring is a topic that has figured prominently in the literature on succession planning and talent management. A mentor is simply a teacher. The first mentor was Nestor, the kindly old man who oversaw the upbringing of Telemachus—Prince of Ithaca and son of King Odysseus—in Homer's *Odyssey*. Mentors are those who informally teach others and do not expect personal gain to result from what they do. For that reason, an immediate supervisor should not be a mentor.

Mentoring is necessary to pass on social relationships. Mentors make introductions between their social contacts and likely successors. Their goal is to ensure that meaningful social relationships persist after they leave.

Both mentors and mentees require training to perform best. While some people are born mentors, it is best not to leave it to chance. Offer some instruction on what mentors should do and what mentees should do. Build the right expectations and skills to make the process work more efficiently.

Step 5: Manage a Process of Social Introductions and Relationship Building

Once the mentors and mentees have been matched up, make sure that they get along with each other. Also ensure that mentors introducing their mentees to those contacts who can affect business results. It is usually best if mentors include mentees in their interactions with their social contacts so that trust can be established over time. Social relationships have not been established until both parties feel comfortable with each other—and can depend on each other.

Step 6: Evaluate the Results Periodically and Make Midcourse Corrections as Necessary

Someone in the organization must monitor the progress of social relationship building efforts. That is often someone in HR, but it does not need to be. Anyone can be assigned to audit how the social relationships are being established and whether those relationships are, in fact, being effectively established. Periodic reports from mentors are helpful in evaluating the results. When need be, midcourse corrections may be made by finding new contacts or establishing new mentors to undertake introductions.

METHODS TO PRESERVE SOCIAL CONTACTS AS WORKERS PREPARE TO RETIRE

No single method should be used to do social relationship succession planning. The reason is that no one method will pick up all social relationships. One size does not fit all. Hence, several methods should be used in combination.

First, adapt the critical incident method for use with social relationship succession planning. Various versions of the critical incident method work for competency modeling, knowledge transfer, and employment branding. It is just that the way questions are asked may have to be different.

To surface important social contacts, use these questions with individuals who are at risk of retirement and who occupy positions of importance to organizational performance.

Think about the most important person inside or outside the company you have ever met who has helped you in your work and in your job at this company.

- What happened in the situation?
- What makes that person so important to your success?
- What special skills or competencies does that individual possess, based on your experience with him or her?
- How can that person be reached? (What is his or her name and contact information?)
- Would it be possible for you to arrange an introduction between another person in our company and that individual to explore mutual and future relationships relevant to the company's needs in the future?
- Would you feel willing to serve as a mentor and adviser in that relationship?

Second, establish communities of practice around key issues affecting the organization. Choose both onsite and online methods to foster information sharing—and relationship building. Post questions online to surface the names of social contacts that can be especially helpful in dealing with specific problems or issues faced by the organization. Then capture the names posted and keep track of them for future use.

To foster onsite communication and social bridge building, host receptions to which social contacts can be invited or can phone in. Encourage participation by would-be mentors and would-be mentees. Emphasize the purpose of the meetings/receptions.

Undoubtedly, other approaches could be used. Often, such social contacts will figure prominently in mentoring programs and that is one reason to establish and maintain such programs in organizations. Be sure to advise mentors to mention their social contact-sand to ask for introductions to individuals who may be helpful to their future development and work performance.

APPLICATION QUESTIONS

1. How does your organization *presently* take planned steps to transfer knowledge from more- to less-experienced workers? How do you believe that *should* be managed in your organization—and in your work unit, department, or division?
2. Few organizations take planned steps to identify their in-house experts (called *HiPros* to distinguish them from HiPos), so as to catalog what knowledge or specialized expertise might be lost as an organization loses highly knowledgeable people through resignations, retirements, and other losses. Identify the HiPros in your work unit, department, or division who possess specialized institutional memory or knowledge in handling daily work problems. Then make a list of practical steps you could take to encourage them to share their knowledge with others.
3. Few organizations take planned steps to identify individuals who have established special relationships with others outside the organization that help them get results. Identify people in your work unit, department, or division who have established special relationships with distributors, suppliers, customers, or other key stakeholders over the years so as to catalog what special social relationships might be lost as an organization experiences resignations, retirements, and other losses. Identify in your work unit, department, or division those people who possess such social relationships. Then make a list of practical steps you could take to encourage them to introduce others in the organization to those social contacts and build trust.

11

Retaining Talent

Turnover is a perennial problem, even in the midst of a global economic downturn. People with special talent are always in demand because their productivity or other value-added traits exceed their total compensation costs. Many managers persist in the belief that the right people can always be found if the organization is just willing to pay enough. And few people doubt that turnover is costly. While studies of the costs of turnover vary, most everyone agrees that if a manager leaves the company, it may cost the equivalent of at least 150 percent of that person's yearly salary to replace him or her.[1]

Misconceptions persist globally about why workers leave their employers. As a 2007 study concluded, "efforts by companies to limit turnover appear to be hampered by an incomplete understanding of employee priorities. For example, workers rank stress as a top reason they would leave their company, but it is not even among the top five reasons that employers cited. Instead, employers cite insufficient pay and lack of career development and promotion opportunities."[2]

163

Consider: What do the terms *retention* and *turnover* mean? What is involved in holding down the turnover of talented people? What role can managers play—and what role should they play—in retention? This chapter addresses these questions.

DEFINING *RETENTION* AND *TURNOVER*

Retention simply means "holding down turnover." *Traditional turnover* is calculated as the number of voluntary quits in a specific time span—such as a month or year—divided by the total head-count of the organization multiplied by one hundred. *Critical turnover* is a more interesting figure for you as a manager. It is the number of voluntary quits among HiPos in a specific time span divided by the total headcount of HiPos in the organization multiplied by one hundred.

There are other ways to conceptualize specialized turnover. For instance, instead of calling it "critical turnover," *HiPo turnover* could be understood as the number of voluntary quits among HiPos in a specific time span divided by the total headcount of HiPos in the organization multiplied by one hundred; *HiPer turnover* could be understood as the number of voluntary quits among HiPers in a specific time span divided by the total headcount of HiPers in the organization multiplied by one hundred; and HiPro turnover could be understood as the number of voluntary quits among HiPros in a specific time span divided by the total headcount of HiPros in the organization multiplied by one hundred.

Note that turnover can thus focus on the departure of different specialized groups in the organization. If traditional turnover is higher than HiPo, HiPer, or HiPro turnover, then the trend is in the right direction. Why? It simply means that fewer high-quality workers are leaving the organization than average or subpar workers.

These special ways of calculating turnover could also be used in your own area of responsibility. How many HiPos do you have in your division, department, or organization? How many HiPers?

How many HiPros? What is their turnover rate? What special steps have you taken to try to hold down the turnover rate of such talented people?

HOW TO HOLD DOWN THE TURNOVER OF TALENTED PEOPLE

Why do employees leave their employers? Many studies have been conducted to examine that question. See, for example, the author's published instrument, The Organizational Retention Assessment, which catalogs 100 retention best practices.[3] While studies about employee retention may be affected by the employment conditions existing at the time they are conducted, one thing is clear: pay is not the only thing that matters.

Employers serious about holding down turnover should pay close attention to satisfaction and dissatisfaction levels of their employees over stress, pay, promotional opportunities, career development opportunities, and work/life balance. One way to do that is to conduct regular employee climate surveys and then develop improvement plans specifically based on the results. The whole organization can do that, or you could use a simple instrument like the one appearing in Exhibit 11–1 in your own division or department to periodically survey worker attitudes. Another way is to survey the satisfaction levels of only those in targeted and specially talented groups, such as HiPos, HiPers, and HiPros. Then management should pay special attention to improving conditions for those talented people.

What should an employer *not* do? I would say "rely on exit interviews only." While there is nothing wrong with exit interviews per se, they may have problems in how they are conducted and how the results are used. Exit interviews may be especially prone to what researchers call *social desirability bias*. That bias refers to the tendency of people to "say things that are socially acceptable—and remain quiet about things that are not so socially acceptable."

Exhibit 11-1. A Simple Climate Survey

Directions: Please complete the following survey of this organization. Indicate your level of satisfaction with each of the items listed in the left column below by marking the number in the right column. Use this scale:

1 = **Very dissatisfied**
2 = **Dissatisfied**
3 = **Somewhat satisfied**
4 = **Very satisfied**

Conditions in the Organization *How satisfied are you with...*	Your Level of Satisfaction			
	Very dissatisfied **1**	**Dissatisfied** **2**	**Somewhat satisfied** **3**	**Very satisfied** **4**
1 The amount of stress you face	1	2	3	4
2 Your base pay/salary	1	2	3	4
3 Promotional opportunities in the organization	1	2	3	4
4 Career development opportunities	1	2	3	4
5 Work/life balance	1	2	3	4
6 Your immediate supervisor	1	2	3	4
7 Other characteristics of importance to you. (*List them and rate them*)	1	2	3	4
8	1	2	3	4
9	1	2	3	4
10	1	2	3	4

For instance, consider how a typical organization conducts an exit interview. On the last day or during the last week of employment, an HR representative asks a departing employee to participate in a face-to-face exit interview. The HR representative asks many questions, but the key focus is basically on "why are you leaving?" The problem is that employees may be uncertain how they want to answer because they are unsure how the results will be used. Suppose the worker may want to avoid "burning bridges" and so commits to say only things that are socially desirable—such as "I am leaving for a better paying job" or "I am leaving to follow my spouse or significant other to another city." Both those answers are socially desirable and leave the door open for employees to ask their old supervisors for a reference in the future or to come back to the organization to request the old job back. But saying other things—perhaps the truth—may not be so socially desirable. Additionally, the employer has no way to check if the individual really is getting more pay at another employer or is really following his or her spouse to another city. The result is that management may be given bad information and will make bad decisions and take ill-advised actions based on that erroneous information.

The traditional exit interview process may be broken and may never be fixed if it is managed in this way. Perhaps a better way is to wait for three weeks after the employee leaves the organization. Then send a postcard and ask the employee to answer questions about his or her departure on a secure Web site. Provide an incentive, such as a gift certificate that can be obtained only if the person completes the exit interview online. Follow up to increase the response rate. At the same time, ask the immediate supervisor of each departing employee to rate the quality of the person leaving for job performance, potential for promotion, and perhaps level of expertise on special business issues or processes. HR practitioners may also ask if the immediate supervisor knows why the person is leaving. By asking both worker and immediate supervisor, the organization obtains information that can be doublechecked.

WHAT MANAGERS SHOULD DO
TO ENCOURAGE RETENTION

There is an old saying that "workers quit their bosses, not their jobs." And research appears to support that view. In 2007, Florida

State University researchers surveyed 700 people about their jobs and got the following results:[4]

- 39% said their supervisor failed to keep promises.
- 37% said their supervisor failed to give credit when due.
- 31% said their supervisor gave them the "silent treatment" in the past year.
- 27% said their supervisor made negative comments about them to other employees or managers.
- 24% said their supervisor invaded their privacy.
- 23% said their supervisor blames others to cover up mistakes or minimize embarrassment.

Some have even called this Bad Boss Syndrome (BBS).[5] BBS is the tendency for managers to blame others for their own shortcomings—or the consequences of them, such as high absenteeism, tardiness, or turnover.

To avoid BBS, you should keep your promises, give credit when it is due, talk to workers directly when you have a problem with something they did, voice criticism to workers directly and not talk behind their backs to others, avoid the appearance of invading people's privacy, and take the blame when a mistake was really your fault. Periodically ask your workers, either in a staff meeting or in an anonymous survey, how you could improve your own ability as a manager. Take what they say to heart, and take action based on what they tell you.

Of particular importance may be talking to HiPos, HiPers, and HiPros. Take them aside and say that you value their opinions. Then say that you are committed to improving your own abilities. What advice would they have about how you could improve your own ability as a manager? Ask the question orally. Then give people a way to answer the question so that the answer will not be traced back to them, such as by writing something on a piece of paper and turning it in. That step alone may well improve your ability to manage—and go a long way toward impressing workers that you really do want to help them.

Some organizations take steps to give retention a central place, since the leaders know that turnover costs.

APPLICATION QUESTIONS

1. How does your organization *presently* manage retention? Is there a systematic plan in place that covers all employees, or does the employer simply handle the loss of highly talented people on a case-by-case basis?
2. What do you *do* to encourage talented people to stay in your organization? Make a list of specific actions you take.
3. How does your organization manage exit interviews? What steps does your organization take to find out why the best people stay?
4. Suppose you heard through the grapevine that one of your high-potential workers was looking for another job. What would you about it? Why would you do that?

NOTES

1. W. G. Bliss, "Cost of employee turnover," downloaded on 15 January 2009 from http://www.isquare.com/turnover.cfm.

2. See http://www.prnewswire.com/cgi-bin/stories.pl?ACCT=109& STORY=/www/story/10-22-2007/0004686982&EDATE=), downloaded on 15 January 2009.

3. W. Rothwell (2007). Organization retention assessment. In E. Beich, ed., *The 2007 Pfeiffer Annual: Consulting* (pp. 177–188). San Francisco: Pfeiffer.

4. "People quit bosses, not organizations" (2007) at http://www.sfgate. com/cgi-bin/article.cgi?file=/chronicle/archive/2007/01/03/ BUGKBNBRTD1.DTL&type=business), downloaded on 15 January 2009

5. See http://media.abcnews.com/GMA/TakeControlOfYourLife/ story?id=2059783, downloaded on 15 January 2009

12

Working with Diverse People

Many organizations include diversity goals in their talent programs—that is, they seek to increase the representation of protected class workers (such as women, minorities, and others) and alternative workers (such as retirees, consultants, and contingent workers) in their talent base. While that may be a goal at the strategic level, what you, as a manager, do on a daily basis affects the long-term outcomes of that strategy.

And diversity, as a topic, is growing more important. In the United States, minorities are the fastest growing population. According to the U.S. Census Bureau, in 2005, 45 percent of American children under the age of five belonged to minorities, and the minority population of the United States reached 102.5 million in 2007. Growth among Hispanics and Latin Americans accounted for nearly half (1.4 million) of the U.S. population growth in the year between 2005 and 2006.

Americans are not as open to diversity as they would like to believe. Consider that the average American believes that residents of the United States account for about 25 percent of the world's population, when it is actually less than 5 percent. The country has a long way to go toward appreciating and even celebrating the diversity of different cultures and nations.

THE IMPORTANCE OF DIVERSITY

Diversity simply means "differences." It is often associated with "acknowledging, understanding, accepting, valuing, and celebrating differences among people with respect to age, class, ethnicity, gender, physical and mental ability, race, sexual orientation, spiritual practice, and public assistance status."[1] *Celebrating diversity* means appreciating other people for who they are—regardless of factors that have nothing to do with performance, such as race, color, sex, religion, national origin, culture, physical or mental disability, age, sexual orientation, gender identity, veterans' status, or immigration status—and the creative perspectives that different people may bring to a group.

Why is diversity important? For one thing, most experts agree that competitive advantage in the future will depend on innovation and creativity. And yet homogeneous groups, while most efficient in doing routine work, are really ill suited to quantum leaps in productivity improvement. If everyone thinks and acts alike, it is unlikely that the group will come up with creative solutions to challenging problems. Heterogeneous (that is, diverse) groups are much better at that. Hence, managing diversity and cultivating diversity in the work place are keys to the competitive advantage of many organizations today.

HOW MANAGERS SHOULD WORK
WITH DIVERSE PEOPLE

It may not be possible for everyone to overcome a lifetime of bias if they were brought up in households where their parents railed against people who were different from them. But you can and should take steps to manage your behaviors in work place settings and keep any bad thoughts, based on stereotypes, to yourself. That is not only the ethically correct thing to do and the legally required thing to do but, from the standpoint of generating creative solutions to tough problems, the best management action to take.

As a manager, you should do more than pay mere lip service to the differences across individuals and groups. You should also realize that it is a good thing for people to be different. You must speak out and act against discrimination when you see it and encourage a culture of inclusiveness where everyone feels valued. If you do not take the lead in doing that, nobody else will. You can't just leave it up to HR. People watch you as a manager and follow your lead. Be careful how you lead!

First, come to an awareness of what discrimination means. Second, reflect on any biases or prejudices that you may have, perhaps as a result of growing up in less enlightened times, and what you can do to manage them. Third, realize that diversity is not about groups but about individuals. Fourth, recognize the strengths as well as the weaknesses in people—and acknowledge them, build on them, and help others to leverage their strengths and potential to best advantage. Fifth, promote open dialogues. Sixth, and finally, encourage mentoring programs.

HOW CAN MANAGERS EFFECTIVELY BRING OUT THE BEST IN PEOPLE, LEVERAGING THEIR STRENGTHS WHILE ALSO BUILDING THEIR COMPETENCIES FOR THE FUTURE?

Bringing out the best in people is a topical issue. In fact, dealing with people in the work place has been a perennial preoccupation. Consider that many books published in recent years have had titles like *Dealing with People You Can't Stand: How to Bring Out the Best in People at Their Worst* (2002), *Since Strangling Isn't an Option: Dealing with Difficult People—Common Problems and Uncommon Solutions* (1999), *Toxic Coworkers: How to Deal with Dysfunctional People on the Job* (2000), and *The Bully at Work: What You Can Do to Stop the Hurt and Reclaim Your Dignity on the Job* (2000).

The first piece of advice to consider in bringing out the best in people is to *listen* to them. Listen for feelings as well as facts. Research indicates that the average manager listens at only 15 percent efficiency. Why? Think about it. You are talking to a worker and the phone rings, somebody drops by, your blackberry beeps, and a fax comes in—all in the space of a few minutes. With all those distractions, you cannot listen—*really listen on all wavelengths*—to what others say. If you make an effort to listen without distractions, people will start to tell you what they have never told anyone else. And that's what you want if you want to cultivate talent.

The second piece of advice is to recognize that people often don't realize their own strengths. As I like to tell people, you don't notice your greatest personal strength because it comes so easily to you that you think everyone can do that. But they can't. It is not until someone expresses amazement at what you have done that you begin to realize that it is an unusual talent, gift or strength. So, make it a point to notice what people do best, express amazement about it, and then ask them how they could leverage it to advantage. That will get them thinking.

The third piece of advice is to recognize that some exceptionally talented people are really canny about taking risks. They are internally driven to achieve—something that Harvard psychologist David McClelland called *achievement motivation*. They are more driven by the desire to succeed than by the rewards that success brings; they set moderately difficult goals that stretch their abilities but do not break them; and they prefer to get concrete feedback on how they are doing based on their own personal contributions. So, for a manager, that means that you may need to challenge high achievers with difficult but not impossible goals and pay enough attention to give them individualized feedback.

The fourth piece of advice has to do with paying attention to individuals more than the tasks or work they do. People are not just "job holders." They are human beings with strengths and weaknesses. One important characteristic is *self-efficacy*. It has to do with the faith that people have in themselves to achieve results. Some high achievers lack that feeling and doubt themselves all the time, sometimes because they lack the experience that can give people confidence in themselves. They may need constant reassurance and constant feedback. It should not be confused with low self-esteem —which can also be a problem—which has to do with how people feel about themselves as human beings. Low self-esteem yields feelings of worthlessness; low self-efficacy yields feelings that difficult tasks cannot be accomplished, even when the person has incredible talent.

As a manager, you need to recognize highly talented people who have feelings of inadequacy in their ability to achieve results. The right course of action is not to agree with them, This way you are not serving as an enabler for their sense of inadequacy. Instead, you should build up their confidence by expressing faith in them and their abilities. Help them plan, since low self-efficacy may make it harder for people to plan. Break down a difficult task and give them bite-sized challenges if you can. That will build their self-confidence and their sense of self-efficacy.

APPLICATION QUESTIONS

1. When some managers think of diversity, the first thing that springs to mind is race and gender. But another way to express it has to do with simple "differences." How do you feel about differences in viewpoints? Value systems? Morals? What should you

do when one of your best workers disagrees with you? How should you handle that?

2. Just how much diversity can you stand? Suppose an exceptionally qualified male job applicant came to a job interview with you dressed in "casual attire" (sweater, jeans, and sneakers) and had long, unkempt hair. Would that affect your perceptions of the applicant? Why?

3. Describe a situation in which a worker reporting to you had a viewpoint different from your own. How did you deal with it?

4. Explain the diversity that presently exists in your area of responsibility. What "differences" are apparent? How do they affect your actions as a manager?

NOTE

1. Esty, Katharine, Richard Griffin, and Marcie Schorr-Hirsh (1995). *Workplace Diversity. A Managers Guide to Solving Problems and Turning Diversity into a Competitive Advantage* (Avon, MA: Adams Media Corporation, 1995).

13

Corrective Action and Decruiting

Managing talent is not just about managing the best people. It can also be about managing the worst ones. Workers watch how their supervisors handle difficult people and bad performers. What happens may influence their behavior.

Most managers, research suggests, devote about 20 percent of their time to managing conflict. That includes solving problems with workers. And yet those same studies indicate that only 10 percent of managers effectively deal with that conflict.[1]

Managers around the world complain that is impossible, or nearly so, to fire poor performers. A possible reason is that many organizations use progressive disciplinary systems that require managers to provide, before termination, an oral warning, a written warning, and sometimes a suspension (in that order) for problem behaviors. Terminated employees may have the right to appeal to internal management committees and/or union committees and then to governmental bodies to seek redress for terminations. Concerns about litigation for discrimination or the public relations complications stemming from a dismissal for cause can complicate management action. Nor can managers defend their actions because of employee privacy laws. Hence, managers sometimes feel that terminating a poor performer can take *years*.

And yet isn't it fair to say that managing poor performers (PoPos) is just as important a test of talent management as managing HiPos, HiPers, and HiPros? Indeed, how an organization's managers handle poor performers is sometimes regarded as a way to measure the quality of management, and how well managers can handle corrective action with problem performers also says much about their ability to manage. Yet employee attitude survey data consistently show across many organizations that large numbers—usually more than half—of employees do not feel that their managers handle poor performers or various troublemakers as effectively, decisively, quickly, or firmly as they should.

DEFINING *CORRECTIVE ACTION* AND *DECRUITMENT*

Corrective action, sometimes referred to by the less positive term *employee discipline,* refers to the process of rectifying problems. The term corrective action is usually preferred to discipline because the focus should be on identifying and addressing the root causes of problematic employee behavior rather than on punishment.

Decruitment is the opposite of recruitment. It simply refers to any means by which worker employment is terminated. It thus includes actions taken with individuals or with groups. Firing one worker is a decruitment action. Similarly, offering workers attractive severance packages to leave the organization—or early retirement packages, lump sum bonuses for quitting, or involuntary layoffs or "smartsizings"—are group-oriented actions to terminate employment. They are all forms of decruitment, and they can all be ways by which to manage talent as well. Use the form in Exhibit 13–1 to help you think about managing your staff and identifying what staff members might be priorities for consideration in a layoff.

Exhibit 13-1. A Form for Classifying Your Staff

Directions: Use this form to help you classify people who report directly to you. In completing this form, place no more than 10 percent of your workers as HiPos (upper left cell of the grid below) and no more than 80 percent of your workers as solids (middle and lower left cell of the grid below). The remaining workers should be classified in one of the other cells of this grid. Write the names of your direct reports right into the cells. Remember that "performance" refers to how well they do their present jobs and "potential" refers to how well suited you believe they would be to be promoted.

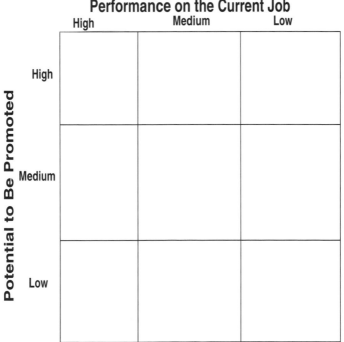

TYPICAL REASONS FOR CORRECTIVE ACTION AND DECRUITMENT

As you probably know, workers can do many things to get under your skin. Some are simply irritating; others may be grounds for corrective action or even immediate termination. Although you, as a manager, may dislike firing people almost as much as you might loathe the idea of death, it is a necessary evil to be familiar with.

Typical reasons for corrective action and/or termination of employment include:

- Lying about or misrepresenting experience, education, or qualifications.
- Obsolescence of the job.
- Poor worker performance.
- Negligence.
- Violation of company policy.
- Violation of safety rules.
- Excessive tardiness.
- Excessive absenteeism.
- Damaging company property.
- Theft.
- Sabotage.
- Sexual harassment.
- Violence or fighting on the job.
- Gambling.
- Possession or use of alcohol or illegal drugs while on the job.
- Sleeping on the job.
- Conviction for a crime.

Of course, employers should consult legal counsel before taking any involuntary dismissal action because legally defensible reasons for termination may vary by country, state, county, or city.

Employers in the United States generally hold to *at-will employment,* the principle that workers can be terminated for a good reason, a bad reason, or no reason. The same principle applies to workers. Indeed, workers can quit their jobs, strike, or even cease work for good reasons, bad reasons, or no reasons.

There are exceptions to at-will employment, however. Notable examples include discrimination based on a long list of protections (such as age, race, ethnic origin, and sexual orientation). Forty-two U.S. states and the District of Columbia also consider a *public policy exception* to at-will employment, in which employers may not fire workers if it violates the state's public policy or a state or federal statute. And, in addition, 38 U.S. states recognize an *implied contract* as an exception to at-will employment, which means that an employer may not fire an employee when an implied contract is formed between an employer and employee, even though no express, written instrument regarding the employment relationship exists.

Other reasons an employer may not use to fire an at-will employee are:

- *Refusing to break the law* – Employers cannot fire employees because they refuse to commit an illegal act.
- *Family or medical leave* – Federal law permits most employees to take a leave of absence for specific family or medical problems. An employer is not permitted to fire an employee who takes family or medical leave for a reason outlined in the Family and Medical Leave Act (FLMA).
- *Not complying with the company's termination procedures* – Often, the employee handbook or company policy outlines a procedure that must be followed before an employee is terminated. If the employer fires an employee without following this procedure, the employee may have a claim for wrongful termination.

Of course, additional complications in firing may exist when the employer is unionized. When that is the case, you will have to follow procedures outlined in existing labor contracts or collective bargaining agreements.

HOW CORRECTIVE ACTION SHOULD BE CARRIED OUT

Before you apply corrective action to any worker, you should ask yourself seven important questions.

1. Was the employee warned in advance of the likely consequence of breaking a rule or otherwise failing to comply with company expectations? (Is there evidence that workers know a rule exists and what might happen if they break it?)
2. Is the rule or company expectation related to the reasonable conduct of the business? (In other words, is it really necessary?)
3. Have you made an effort to investigate the facts? (In other words, have you taken steps to find out what really happened and avoided taking someone's word for it?)
4. Did your investigation yield strong evidence that the worker actually did break the rule? (Or is it unclear what happened?)
5. How serious was the problem? (In short, how important was or is it to company performance?)
6. How does the problem compare to past problems, if any, with this worker? Is it a first offense? Or is part of a pattern of problem behaviors?
7. How does the proposed action with this worker compare to other actions taken with other workers for the same problem? (In short, is there consistency in the way that corrective action is applied?)

If you still decide to proceed with corrective action, then follow seven key steps.

1. Clarify specifically what happened. Get the facts clear. Put it in writing, if possible.
2. Clarify specifically what is expected or what should be happening. In short, describe the rule that was broken or the standard that must be met.
3. Describe the difference between what happened and what should be happening, laying out the facts in clear, specific and, if possible, measurable terms.
4. Emphasize the consequences or impact of the problem behavior. How does it affect the company or other people?
5. Meet with the employee. Start in a positive, action-oriented way. Ask for the employee's cooperation in solving a problem. State the purpose of the meeting and provide the written documentation. (Putting things in writing is always desirable, both because it increases the impact of the meeting and forces you to think it out.)
6. State any punishment that you are giving.
7. Describe what changes you expect to happen. Provide coaching on how those changes should be made; provide a reasonable period for compliance; and, clarify what will happen upon the next occurrence.

Use the Worksheet in Exhibit 13–2 to guide your documentation of corrective action.

BILL'S TIP – CORRECTIVE ACTION
You have many options as a manager in taking corrective action. You can:

- Issue a verbal warning.
- Give a written warning.
- Withhold pay increases.
- Suspend with or without pay.

- Demote a worker.
- Reassign the worker.
- Dismiss the worker.

Exhibit 13-2. Corrective Action Form

Directions: Complete the following corrective action form. Give a copy to the employee, and place a copy in his or her personnel file—or else scan it and place on file for the employee. Add paper and attach to this form if necessary.

Name of Employee	Name of Supervisor/Person Completing This Form
Today's Date	Type of Correction Action (check a box below √) □ Verbal Warning □ Written Warning □ Termination Notification
Documentation	
1. What happened that prompted the need for this corrective action? (*Describe specifically what happened, citing date[s], time[s] and nature of event[s].*)	
2. What should the employee have done? (*Describe specifically what policy or law, rule or regulation was violated or the nature of the problem behavior.*)	
3. What was the consequence or impact of the difference between the answers to questions 1 and 2 above?	
4. What should the employee do in the future, and what specific coaching advice do you have to offer the employee to improve?	
5. How much time are you giving the employee to improve?	
6. What will happen if this problem or this behavior happens again?	
Supervisor's Signature and Date	**Worker's Signature and Date**
	I have read and understand this form, but my signature does not necessarily mean that I agree with this corrective action.
_____/_____ **Signature** **Date**	_____/_____ **Signature** **Date** □ **Worker chooses not to sign**

The corrective action meeting is very important. You will probably get an indication of what will happen with the situation based on the tenor of the meeting. If the worker agrees to cooperate, the chance is much greater that improvement will occur. But if the worker resists, then the chance of improvement is diminished.

Watch for predictable defenses. Typically, employees who are "called on the carpet" will defend themselves in several common ways. Be ready for these. First, the employees will claim that they did not do what they are accused of doing. Have your facts straight, and refute that with your evidence. Second, employees may claim that they were never informed of the rule or the performance standard. Refute that by having employees sign, during onboarding, for employee handbooks or policy manuals that stipulate these rules and performance management plans that set forth measurable key performance indicators. Third, employees may claim that they were trained improperly. If you ask for documentation of on-the-job training, such as a checklist that was initialed by trainer and trainee, you can refute that charge. Fourth, and finally, employees are likely to complain that they are being unfairly singled out for a problem that other workers are also guilty of. Refute that by saying "the discussion

---

BILL'S TIP – CORRECTIVE ACTION

Take special care in taking corrective action and ask for help from the HR department and/or the legal department if a worker:

- Is a member of a protected class.
- Is pregnant.
- Recently filed a claim for workers' compensation.
- Complained of safety issues, sexual harassment, or discrimination.
- Is facing a pending problem with illness or divorce.
- Is experiencing mental or physical problems that could be protected under the Americans with Disabilities Act.

here focuses on you only. I will address problems with other employees with them directly." Keep the focus on the person receiving corrective action. Finally, it may be wise to have a witness present—such as a member of HR—to jump in to help you if you are concerned about charges of unfair discrimination. Document the conversation.

HOW DECRUITMENT SHOULD BE HANDLED

Decruitment includes both terminations for cause and separations, such as layoffs or downsizing dismissals that may be temporary or permanent. Each deserves separate treatment, and so a different section below is addressed to each of these scenarios.

Terminating an Employee for Cause

Before terminating an employee, you should make sure that it comes as no big surprise. In fact, firing someone by surprise can lead to ugly confrontations that could be avoided if corrective action has been properly carried out in advance. So, be sure that the termination meeting comes as no surprise. The worker should have been informed—preferably multiple times—what was expected, how the worker has been performing or behaving, what you advise to correct the problem, how much time is to be permitted for correction, and what consequences will stem from lack of improvement.

> **BILL'S TIP – CORRECTIVE ACTION**
>
> A fundamental principle of corrective action is that workers must have had adequate warning. That means they know ahead of time that they are breaking a rule. It is your job to make sure they know rules ahead of time. If you say you are too busy to do that, then don't be surprised when your hands are tied in corrective action.

Take some time—like a day or two—to think about it and prepare all relevant documents. Inform your own supervisor, the legal office, and the HR department in advance so that they can give you any last-minute words of wisdom and so that they are not caught by surprise if the worker appeals to them. Alert security because the help of that office, on rare occasions, may be necessary. Then move quickly—and do not change your mind, waver, or decide to give the person a second chance after you have begun the firing process. Write a letter of termination, documenting the facts as you see them and indicating the termination. Inform the worker that he or she is being terminated. Have the worker's password revoked just before the meeting, but do that in confidence. Escort the person (or ask security officers to do so) to his or her cubicle to remove belongings—or else have that taken care of so that the worker does not have time to return to the work area. Ask for keys and any other company property that the employee still possesses. Explain how you will send the final severance check to the worker. Document everything said. If asked by other workers why the employee was terminated, remember that you cannot set forth what happened due to employee privacy laws. Therefore, you will have to remain silent about the specific reasons for the termination.

Use the checklist appearing in Exhibit 13–3 as a tool to help you plan how to carry out a termination. Of course, you should double check the form with your organization's HR and legal staffs to ensure that it matches up to your organization's existing policies and procedures and to the laws, rules, and regulations of the location where your work is conducted.

Laying Off a Worker or Group of Workers

Layoffs are part of the modern business scene. They happen all the time. And they are not always well managed—or used to advantage.

The most common mistake is to hold a "Friday afternoon massacre." In that scenario, everyone who is to be laid off is called into a

Exhibit 13-3. A Checklist to Guide Employee Termination

Directions: Use this checklist as a starting point to help you plan an employee termination. (It is important that you plan such a termination.) For each item appearing in the left column below, indicate whether you have done it or not (or whether it is not applicable). Make any notes about what you may need to do in the right column. You should probably meet with representatives of the HR department and/or the legal department before holding a termination meeting.

Plans for Termination *Have you*:	Response			Notes
	Yes	No	Not applicable	
1 Reviewed the company's policies on employee discipline and corrective action to ensure that you have complied with the procedures set forth by the organization?				
2 Made sure that the termination comes as no surprise because the worker has had adequate warning in advance?				
3 Prepared all documents relating to the action in advance, such as previous documentation?				
4 Informed your own supervisor, the HR department, and the legal department that the termination is pending?				
5 Alerted the security department of the pending termination so as to be prepared for the unlikely event of a disturbance?				

6	Alerted the IT department about what to do about the employee's password and access to computer equipment?				
7	Inventoried the employee's equipment and other company resources, such as keys, so that you can go through and check them off as they are returned?				
8	Decided what to do about moving the employee's belongings from his or her office/cubicle before the time comes?				
9	Prepared a written letter that sets forth the causes for the termination and had it reviewed in advance by others (such as your superior, HR and/or legal)?				
10	Decided how to handle the employee's severance check and the employee's rights to insurance (COBRA)?				
11	Carefully planned the time and place of the termination so that it is conducted in a private place?				
12	Considered how to reallocate the worker's duties and tasks so that they can be reassigned as soon as he or she is gone?				

(continued)

Exhibit 13-3. Continued

Plans for Termination *Have you*:		Response			Notes
		Yes	No	Not applicable	
13	Planned exactly how to communicate about the worker's departure to other workers without going into the reasons (due to employee privacy issues)?				
14	Planned for the quick departure of the employee from the work setting after the termination?				
15	Remembered anything else that should be managed that was not listed above? If so, list them here and describe:				

room on Friday afternoon. Unless care is taken, the word has already leaked, and everyone knows what is about to happen. It can get ugly.

A second common mistake is that managers take pains to plan the layoff, but forget to plan the reallocation of work on the following Monday morning. The result is that the most productive workers jump in (or are forced by others to jump in) and take over work that is falling through the cracks, but they are not at all happy because (in most cases) their own pay has not been increased and they are rarely recognized for their extra contribution. When this happens, the best people start looking for other jobs, and when each of them leaves it is like losing 20 people.

A third common mistake is to focus on the layoff and forget alternatives. Are there other ways that these workers can be used in the organization? Is there any chance they can be transferred, moved to telecommuting work, or otherwise continued in employment in some capacity? Consider those options first.

A fourth common mistake is to fail to take full advantage of layoffs. They can be used to shed poor performers or unredeemable troublemakers. You should try to do that when a layoff is unavoidable. Of course, on occasion that is impossible—in organizations with collective bargaining agreements, for instance, that specify how layoff decisions will be made.

Watch out for these common mistakes and take care to avoid them if you can. But, if the layoff is still necessary, then plan carefully for it.

Here is another list of things not to do:

- Don't allow people to be confused. Tell people they are laid off in the first sentence.
- Deliver messages in person and not by impersonal means, such as e-mail.
- Don't make remarks like, "I'm sorry I have to do this to you." Just focus on what is happening.
- Don't open with small talk like, "How are your kids?"
- Don't insult the person in an apparent attempt to rationalize by making yourself feel better about what you are doing.
- Don't mention who else is being laid off.
- Don't say, "You must feel terrible, and I can understand that." Keep the tone action oriented.

So, what should you do? The best approach is to call a meeting about midweek that is not near a major holiday. Keep it under wraps. Have it all carefully planned and orchestrated. Be sure that HR, your own manager, the legal division, and security have all been notified—but have also been sworn to secrecy. Check with the legal and HR departments to ensure that all legal requirements for the layoff have been met. If possible, meet individually with the workers to be laid off. Keep the meeting short—about 15 minutes. Explain the reasons for the layoff and whether it is likely to be permanent or temporary (but do not make a promise of continued employment). Have final checks prepared and hand them out. Be ready to give workers information about insurance and vacation or sick time in writing. Ask for company property back and have an inventory, prepared in advance, of who has what. It is desirable that people leave at the time of the lay off and don't hang around for days or a week after your discussion, since they are likely to be disgruntled. Be prepared to handle security passwords as workers leave the premises so that they cannot gain access from home. Be polite, tactful, and firm. It is not your fault; it is the company's situation that has prompted the layoff. Remember that.

APPLICATION QUESTIONS

1. Describe the typical problems you face in dealing with your workers on a daily basis. Then describe how you manage them. How well do you think you handle people who are chronically late for work? Absent regularly on Mondays or Fridays? Do not perform as well as other workers? Now describe how you feel you could improve the way you handle those employee problems?

2. How do you think high-potential workers might feel if they see a worker "get away with murder," and they feel nothing is done about it? How might that influence their own behavior?

3. Tell a story about the most challenging situation you ever faced in dealing with a difficult worker. Answer these questions: (1) What happened? (Answer that question in some detail but avoid giving the names of current employees); (2) What did you

do about the situation, and what happened as a result of what you did? (3) How long ago did this happen? (4) Where did this happen? (5) What happened as a result of what you did, and how would you handle the situation in the future based on what you learned from this experience?

4. Tell a story about the most common daily problem you face with workers in your area of responsibility. Single out just one example, and answer these questions: (1) What typically happens? (Answer that question in some detail but avoid giving the names of current employees); (2) What do you do about the situation, and what happens as a result of what you do? (3) How often do you face this problem? (4) What advice would you give others who face similar situations?

NOTE

1. Maureen Moriarty (2007) Workplace Coach: Few managers handle conflict effectively, from http://seattlepi.nwsource.com/business/325554_workcoach30.html?source=mypi, accessed on 16 January 2009.

14

Self-Development

The best leader—and the best manager—is one who sets a good example. This chapter addresses the importance to managers of developing themselves—and trying to do that every day, rather than once a year or just when time permits. This chapter offers some practical advice on continuous self-development. Think of it as continuous improvement of yourself!

DEFINING SELF-DEVELOPMENT

Self-development is the continuous process of developing oneself by building your competencies and realizing your potential. You cannot effectively build talent in others if you cannot do it for yourself. It occurs on and off the job, through planned and unplanned learning. It is not restricted to classrooms or to formal training. You can learn by whom you work for, whom you work with, what you do, how you do it, where you do it, how much time pressure you experience, and even your failures.

BILL'S TIP – SELF-DEVELOPMENT

What competencies typify a manager who is effective at self-development? According to a 1973 article by Charles Scheips,[2] a manager who is successful at self-development:

- Has developed self-insight.
- Has become people oriented.
- Has developed personal public relations.
- Assumes rather than merely accepts responsibility.
- Becomes a calculated risk taker.
- Is results oriented.
- Becomes a generalist rather than remains a specialist in skills.
- Is identified with organizational goals.

Some people have to learn to solve a specific problem they face, whether in their lives or on their jobs. Some people learn for the sheer love of acquiring new knowledge and skills. Some people learn because they like to work with other people. Some people learn because they are preparing themselves for future challenges— or in hopes of future, higher earnings. Some people learn for a combination of all these reasons. Why do *you* learn?

THE IMPORTANCE OF SELF-DEVELOPMENT

There are at least six reasons why self development is important for you as a manager.

First, evidence suggests that people who value self-development and learning tend to be more successful and lead more satisfying, happier, and more fulfilling lives than those who do not. Hence, loving self-development can lead to happiness.

Second, the half-life of all human knowledge is on the decline. Due to the world wide Web and the Internet, and more recently the advent of Web 2.0 which encourages social networking and interaction, all human knowledge is turning over about once every 10 years or less. That means it is essential to keep learning just to keep one's knowledge, skills, and abilities current.

Third, self-development is essential to help meet your organization's business needs. You owe your employer your thinking skills and your judgment. If you lack current knowledge, skills, and abilities, then you cannot possibly give your employer the benefit of your thinking because your thinking is possibly based on outdated information.

Fourth, self-development is important because you set an example for your employees. They watch your every move. You can be a respected role model. If you do not take steps to develop yourself, you can hardly expect them to do so enthusiastically. They will not. They watch what you do as well as how you talk.

Fifth, self-development is important to keep yourself marketable. Even though you may have no intention of leaving your organization, you may find that in the current, fiercely competitive global marketplace, companies come and go. You could lose your job through no fault of your own. You must always keep your skills current so that you are not long on the job search if your company should go bankrupt, be acquired, or merged.

Sixth, and finally, self-development is intimately linked with learning. Some research suggests that high-potential workers differ from other workers because they have superior learning ability. The best way to learn how to learn is to keep doing it. Practice improves the skill. So, commit to develop yourself continuously so as to make yourself a high potential and thereby increase your opportunities on your current job, or in higher-level jobs, in the future.

HOW TO CARRY OUT SELF-DEVELOPMENT

You should plan your self-development the same way you approach a business challenge or a major project. Start by deciding what you must learn and/or what would be merely useful to learn about.

A good place to start is by consulting the competency models for your level in the organization and for higher levels. Carefully examine the behavioral indicators in those models. If necessary, informally initiate your own 360-degree assessment; if you must, do it formally. Ask peers, subordinates, and immediate superiors what they believe you are best at—and what you could improve on.

Then plan to leverage your strengths and reduce the impact of your weaknesses.

Leverage your strengths by thinking about how you could serve as a mentor to others. Take steps to teach others what you know. That is your legacy. You can leverage your strengths by teaching others so that they get better.

Reduce the impact of your weaknesses by identifying them, preferably based on the specific language found in the behavioral indicators associated with your organization's competency models, and then asking someone you approach as a mentor what priorities to set. You could approach those your admire, respect, or trust from inside or outside your own organization. Share with them what you would like to learn, and then ask for advice on how to approach that learning process. Do they know people who are particularly good at what you want to learn? Do they know places—called "centers of excellence"—inside or outside the company where you could learn more? Can they suggest specific work assignments inside or outside the company that could build your competencies? Can they suggest learning events, such as training courses, conferences, or other resources, including books or articles, for you to consult for more information?

Develop your own individual development plan even if your organization does not require one. Be sure to clarify:

- What you want to learn and why.
- How it relates to your organization and its strategic objectives.
- How it relates to your career goals and your personal life objectives.
- How you will go about the learning process (specify things to do).
- When you will complete the learning experience(s).
- How you will evaluate the relative success of your learning experiences.

Document this plan in writing. Do not necessarily expect to receive encouragement or support from your own immediate supervisor or from your own organization. One test of your own commitment is whether you are willing to take vacation time to meet your learning plans and are willing to spend money from your own pocket to do so. (Of course, it is wonderful if you do obtain support from your employer.)

Use the Worksheet in Exhibit 14–1 to organize and document your own thoughts about self-development.

Take the initiative to find yourself a mentor. Pick someone whose opinion you respect. Often that person will be someone other

---

BILL'S TIP – SELF-DEVELOPMENT

To be effective in self-development, you must:

- *Take responsibility for it.* Don't say ,"I don't have time." You always have time for what is important.
- *Realize that self-development does not just occur in classes.* It can occur by reading books, talking to other people, listening to audiotapes, and watching videos.

Exhibit 14-1. A Personal Development Plan

Directions: Use this form as a personal development planning form. If your organization uses Individual Development Plans (IDPs), you may not need this form. But it may be useful to prompt some deep self-reflection. For each question appearing in the left column below, write some notes to yourself in the right column below. Review this plan periodically to reflect more on "where you are going in your career and in your life." Add paper as necessary.

Questions	Answers
1	What do you most want out of your life? Your career? Why do you want those?	
2	What is your career goal in the short term (1-3 years) and in the long term (beyond 3 years)? How do your career goals relate to your life goals (such as your marriage, desired age of retirement, etc.)?	
3	What do you want or need to learn that would help you realize your career goal in the short term and in the long term?	
4	How does your wanted or needed learning relate to your organization and its strategic objectives?	
5	How will you build your competencies through learning, and what specific kind of learning do you believe would be helpful? (Remember that there is more to development than "taking training." You can learn from other people, work assignments, self-initiated learning experiences, mentors, places you work or visit, and much more)	

6	When you will complete the learning experience(s)? What are your time lines for learning? Your milestones?	
7	How will you evaluate the relative success of your learning experiences?	

than your own immediate supervisor, since your own supervisor has a selfish stake in your future. But you want someone who will give you advice for your own benefit. So, for that reason, it is often wise to pick someone other than your immediate supervisor. Approach that person—or people, since it is often wise to have several mentors —and ask if he, she, or they will mentor you. Take them to lunch or dinner, pay the bill, and ask for help. Set forth your plan and get their advice. Then document what is said, reflect on it seriously, and carry it out.

Review your personal plan at least once a year—and preferably every quarter. Decide if goals or priorities have changed and if the same approaches can be used to build competencies and evaluate the results. Manage your own development with exactly the same tough mindset you would use in managing a project. It is primarily to your benefit, and not anyone else's, that you do so.

PRESENTING A ROLE MODEL FOR SELF-DEVELOPMENT ON A DAILY BASIS

It is not enough for you to develop yourself. You must show others—your own workers—that you are doing so. When they see you taking the initiative to learn, you will be setting an example that will be tough for even your most cynical worker to make fun of. They will figure that if you are serious about it for yourself, then they should be as well.

Another thing you can do is to open every staff meeting by asking your direct reports what they have done that day or week to develop themselves or others. That will build awareness of how important it is. You can also take that opportunity to reemphasize why taking initiative to develop oneself and others is so critically important.

APPLICATION QUESTIONS

1. What kind of role model for self-development are you? How often do workers see you taking steps to keep your skills current and to improve yourself?
2. How assertive are you in taking the initiative to seek out challenges to increase your skills and build your competencies? How could you improve in that regard?
3. How much encouragement do you receive from your own supervisor in keeping your skills current and improving yourself? What does your own supervisor do that encourages or discourages your own willingness to improve yourself? Do you follow the example set by your own supervisor in dealings with your own employees?
4. Imagine for a moment that you had the ability to get any kind of development that you think would help you prepare for your own advancement. What would that be? How much of it would be on-the-job and how much would be off-the-job? How supportive would your own supervisor be to encouraging you to follow through to do what you think might develop you?

Appendix I

Frequently Asked Questions About Talent Management

QUESTION 1: WHY IS TALENT MANAGEMENT IMPORTANT NOW?

Talent management is important today for several reasons.

First, the global population is aging. The so-called Baby Boom generation, not limited to the United States, is preparing to exit the work force through retirement. After years of downsizing, many organizations will not have enough seasoned middle managers developed to fill expected senior management openings or enough seasoned front-line supervisors to fill expected middle management openings.

In the United States, the Baby Boomers represent 28 percent of the population. According to Bill Geist's book, *The Big 5-Oh,* a Baby Boomer turns 50 every 7 seconds.[1] That means about 10,000 people per day will become eligible for retirement over the next 20 years. So what? Consider that approximately one-half of all senior executives in the Fortune 500 are presently retirement eligible. Since there is a correlation between compensation level and willingness to retire when eligible, it means that a huge number of people are ready to exit the global work force. And they represent the top of the organizational pyramid. When they leave, they create a *domino effect* in which filling a senior vacancy from within leads to a middle management vacancy, which, in turn, can lead to a supervisory vacancy. That, in turn, can lead to a front line worker vacancy. About 50 percent of all U.S. government workers are presently retirement eligible and that means that the government may be competing for exactly the same talent as businesses.

Second, talented people are always in short supply. We may be able to hang up a "help wanted sign," put an ad in the newspaper, or list an opening on a Web-based site, but that does not mean we will find exceptionally talented—and also *promotable*—workers to fill the vacancies. Although everyone has talent, that does not mean that we can find the people whose talent best matches up to the present and future needs of our organizations.

The real talent shortage, according to some business observers, is leadership talent. Many organizations have people occupying high-level spots on the organization chart, but that does not guarantee they are great leaders, who are capable of inspiring workers, growing the business, attracting and keeping customers, or developing people.

Third, the inability to attract, develop, and retain people may be a hindrance to business growth and continuity. According to McKinsey, a global consulting company,[2] the need for superior talent is increasing, but many big U.S. companies are fighting—and losing—the war to attract and retain it. A 2 percent economic growth rate for 15 years would increase the demand for executives by about a third. Meanwhile, supply is moving in the opposite direction: the number of U.S. 35- to 44-year-olds will decline by 15 percent from 2000 to 2015. Companies must therefore make talent management a top priority, create and perpetually refine their employee value proposition, and source and, above all, develop talent systematically while removing underperformers.

A contributing factor is the *skills gap,* which shows that recent graduates lack the abilities needed by businesses. According to the Workforce Alliance: "'Baby boom' retirements, flat population growth and stagnant workforce investment could, by 2010, leave 5.3 million skilled U.S. jobs without skilled U.S. workers to fill them."[3]

Fourth, the world can be a dangerous place. Such natural disasters as hurricanes, tornadoes, typhoons, earthquakes, and floods can lead to loss of life of talented people. More people have been injured in recent years as a result of natural disasters because locations prone to such disasters, such as the Florida coast, have experienced significant population growth. Man-made disasters, such as terrorist strikes, can also lead to the loss of life of talented people. According to one source, terrorist attacks have increased by 3,389 percent since the year 2000.[4]

Admittedly, unknown factors influencing talent management include immigration and offshoring. Some business observers claim that there will be no talent shortage because work that could be done in the United States or in other higher wage nations will simply be shipped offshore to lower wage nations, such as China, India, the Philippines, Vietnam, or Thailand—or to even lower cost nations in Africa. Offshoring is on the increase despite the reservations that are often cited.

U.S. immigration policy can be a mitigating factor, but only if it attracts and retains talented immigrants rather than merely low-cost farm labor. Consider what the White House office of economic advisers has to say about immigration's impact on the United States[5]:

- Immigrants are a critical part of the U.S. work force and contribute to productivity growth and technological advancement. They make up 15% of all workers and even larger shares of certain occupations such as construction, food services and health care. Approximately 40% of Ph.D. scientists working in the United States were born abroad. (Source: Bureau of Labor Statistics; American Community Survey)

- Many immigrants are entrepreneurs. The Kauffman Foundation's index of entrepreneurial activity is nearly 40% higher for immigrants than for natives (Source: Kauffman Foundation).
- Immigrants and their children assimilate into U.S. culture. For example, although 72% of first-generation Latino immigrants use Spanish as their predominant language, only 7% of the second generation is Spanish dominant (Source: Pew Hispanic Center/Kaiser Family Foundation).
- Immigrants have lower crime rates than natives. Among men aged 18 to 40, immigrants are much less likely to be incarcerated than natives. (Source: Butcher and Piehl)
- Immigrants slightly improve the solvency of pay-as-you-go entitlement programs such as Social Security and Medicare. The 2007 OASDI Trustees Report indicates that an additional 100,000 net immigrants per year would increase the long-range actuarial balance by about 0.07% of taxable payroll. (Source: Social Security Administration)
- The long-run impact of immigration on public budgets is likely to be positive. Projections of future taxes and government spending are subject to uncertainty, but a careful study published by the National Research Council estimated that immigrants and their descendants would contribute about $80,000 more in taxes (in 1996 dollars) than they would receive in public services. (Source: Smith and Edmonston)

QUESTION 2: WHAT ARE SOME KEY TRENDS AFFECTING TALENT MANAGEMENT?

Several key trends are affecting talent management.

First, organizational leaders are becoming more aware of the need to address talent management. Many leaders look around the senior management table and see only white-haired (or no-haired) male peers. While there may be a natural human tendency to avoid the subjects of succession planning and talent management because it brings to mind one's own mortality, it just makes good business sense to do it. Business, like the show, must go on.

Second, boards of directors are becoming more active about succession planning and related issues. Board members face the challenge of overcoming a CEO's natural tendency to worry that succession planning signals that the board wants to replace the CEO incumbent. But, in reality, it only makes sense for a board to focus on what to do in the event of the sudden loss of the CEO or other key executives. After all, if that should happen, it will fall squarely in the lap of the board to solve—and sometimes that will necessarily mean the need for quick action. Boards increasingly do not want to be caught off guard.

Third, many older workers are staying past traditional retirement age—or are coming back in various positions. The trend is for retirement to be reinvented. Indeed, many organizations are now actively recruiting, developing, and retaining traditional postretirement workers.

Fourth, more software solutions are available to support talent management programs. While software may lighten the load, it does not bring with it "plug-and-play" solutions. Software is no substitute for the hard work on an interpersonal level of recruiting, developing, and retaining talent.

QUESTION 3: WHAT FRAMEWORK SHOULD THE ORGANIZATION ESTABLISH TO SUPPORT TALENT MANAGEMENT IN AN ORGANIZATION?

Managers do not necessarily need a strategic infrastructure to support a talent management program. They can, after all, do it all themselves in methods that range from simple replacement charting to the more elaborate approach of forming committees within departments or divisions to review talent. But it sure helps to have an organization strategic framework in place, so that talent is regarded as an organizational asset rather than each manager's private, individual asset.

See Exhibit A-1 for a strategic framework that illustrates talent management. The model's steps are described below.

Exhibit A-1. A Strategic Framework for Talent Management

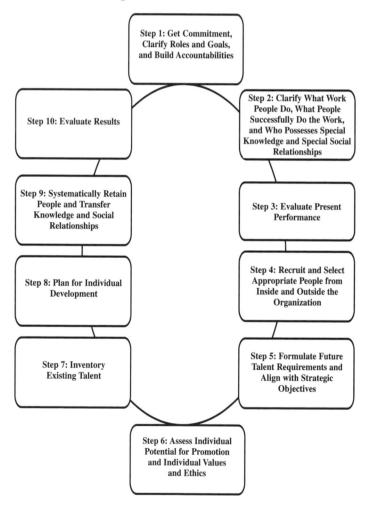

Step 1: Get Commitment, Clarify Roles and Goals, and Build Accountabilities

No talent management effort can thrive unless it enjoys the full commitment of top-, middle-, and lower-level managers. For that reason, an essential first step is securing—and sustaining—management commitment. Managers must do more than pay lip service to talent management. They must demonstrate efforts to support it every day through their actions. They must devote personal time to it.

Each key group of stakeholders in the organization—top managers, middle managers, first-line managers, and workers—have roles to play in the talent management effort. These roles must be clarified and communicated. Further, individuals must be held accountable, and even rewarded, for carrying out their roles and getting results.

Talent management efforts may, of course, have many goals. These must be clarified and prioritized. Managers must agree on them, so that the talent management system does not try to be all things to all people. Typical talent management goals may include the following:

- Preparing sufficiently well-qualified replacements before key leaders retire or are lost due to sudden death, long-term disability, or other unexpected events.
- Preparing sufficient numbers of well-qualified people to support business expansion.
- Recruiting high potentials from outside the organization.
- Developing high potentials inside the organization.
- Role-modeling talent management efforts by developing self and others.

Of course, many such goals may exist. They should be formulated based on business needs and should be measurable. Senior managers must reach agreement on what the goals are and how to measure them.

Step 2: Clarify What Work People Do, What People Successfully Do the Work, and Who Possesses Special Knowledge and Special Social Relationships

It is not possible to implement an effective talent management program if it is not clear what work people do and what kind of people are needed to do the work. Hence, it is necessary to update job descriptions and formulate competency models, which describe the successful people who do the work. Job descriptions must, of course, be tailored to meet the specific needs of the organization. The same principle also applies to competency models, which are influenced by the corporate culture.

Step 3: Evaluate Present Performance

Performance management is essential to any talent management program. While individuals should not be promoted solely because they are performing well in their present jobs, it is also true that they should not be promoted if they are failing their current jobs. Effective performance management programs should measure both results (such as key performance indicators) and the behaviors linked to achieving the results essential to job success.

Step 4: Recruit and Select Appropriate People from Inside and Outside the Organization

There are basically two ways to secure talent—develop it from inside the organization or recruit it from outside. It is thus essential to think creatively to outcompete other organizations in recruiting talent. At the same time, most organizational leaders should review their job posting and other internal recruitment programs to ensure that the best-qualified people are being recruited internally for each vacancy. After all, some managers hoard talent. That is particularly true after widespread downsizing because managers fear that if they lose a good performer to another department to a promotion, they will not be allowed to replace the person at all.

Selection methods should also be examined. On what basis are people being chosen? Are the approaches based on the competencies and behaviors essential to job success? Or, are other and perhaps more subjective criteria being used in selection? A trend in selection is to use multiple methods to judge the suitability of job applicants to demonstrate the competencies and behaviors linked to work success.

Step 5: Formulate Future Talent Requirements and Align Them with Strategic Objectives

Talent requirements do not remain static. As organizational leaders pursue strategic plans, talent requirements must be reviewed periodically to ensure that people are being considered for promotion based on future, rather than merely present, talent requirements. After all, people must be prepared for promotion based on future, not always current, needs. It takes time to develop people. For that reason, it is essential to consider future talent requirements and align them to the organization's strategic objectives.

Step 6: Assess Individual Potential for Promotion and Individual Values and Ethics

Assessing individual potential is all about determining if people can perform at higher responsibility levels. It is commonly called *potential assessment.*[6] Good performers at one level—as measured by systematic performance management—will not necessarily perform well at higher levels of responsibility because different competencies are required. Common approaches to assessing potential include manager nominations, multirater assessments, psychological tests, assessment centers, realistic job tryouts, and work samples. While potential assessment usually focuses on comparing individuals to the competencies required at higher levels of responsibility, recent thinking has suggested that organizational leaders should also measure individuals against corporate values and codes of ethical conduct.

Step 7: Inventory Existing Talent

How quickly and effectively can an organization find its talent in a crisis? Finding talent is often done informally by asking managers, but that is not necessarily an effective, or speedy, approach. And large organizations face a particular challenge because there are so many people, and individuals may possess different talents and may even be in-house experts on specialized business problems. How easy is it to find talent when it is needed? Organizational leaders should thus establish competency inventories, based on the problems faced by the organization, to catalog and find talent quicker. Time is a strategic issue. Finding talent quickly can sometimes spell the difference between competitive success —or failure.

Step 8: Plan for Individual Development

How are individuals groomed for higher levels of responsibility? The most common way is to establish individual development plans (IDPs) to narrow developmental gaps between what competencies people must possess to be qualified for promotion and what competencies they presently possess. Many organizations have established learning management systems (LMSs) that make it easy for individuals to pinpoint appropriate methods to build their competencies. Typically, IDPs indicate what competencies people need to develop, how they will do it, what resources they will use to do it, and how their learning will be measured or otherwise assessed.

Some approaches to developing individuals may be group oriented, such as in-house leadership development programs. Others may be hands-on in which individuals are given specific work or action learning projects that build their competencies while learning from others. Still others can be individualized and may include on-the-job learning or on-the-job coaching.

Step 9: Systematically Retain People and Transfer Knowledge and Social Relationships

Few organizations have systematic retention programs that are geared to keeping the best people. Exit interviews are just not enough. More often retention is handled on a case-by-case basis. Unfortunately, such *ad hoc* approaches usually result in treating some people differently from others, thereby creating ill will and eventually prompting more turnover. What is needed is a consistent organizational approach to retention that makes systematic use of best practices in retention.

Organizational leaders should also take effective steps to transfer the special knowledge of high professionals—sometimes called *in-house experts* or *high professionals (HiPros)*—who are not necessarily promotable but who possess specialized competencies in solving unique problems confronting the organization. Such experts can be highly effective mentors when they are willing to transfer some of what they know, or have learned from experience, to others.

Finally, organizational leaders should also take steps to transfer social relationships. That is highly challenging. Many people have established a broad social network to help them do their jobs. For instance, some salespeople are highly effective in finding the best people to make decisions on sales. When these salespeople leave the organization for retirement, these social contacts are lost. But it is not as simple as making introductions; rather, customers and others must learn to trust successors. It is thus necessary to groom successors through a series of projects so that customers learn to trust them. Of course, social relationships can also exist in occupations outside sales, and they are just as important to transfer to successors.

Step 10: Evaluate Results

Evaluating talent management programs is a topical issue. Many executives and HR practitioners wonder how to evaluate talent programs. Effective talent management programs, however, are evaluated by metrics established from the initial goals identified for the program. Suppose, for instance, that a goal of a talent program is to groom successors in preparation for a wave of expected top management retirements. In that example, it would (of course) be appropriate to measure the program based on how many and how well individuals are prepared to meet that goal. That can be tracked annually.

QUESTION 4: WHAT ROLES IN TALENT MANAGEMENT SHOULD BE PLAYED BY THE ORGANIZATION'S CEO, TOP MANAGERS, MIDDLE AND FRONT-LINE MANAGERS, HR DEPARTMENT, AND INDIVIDUALS?

To move beyond strategic-level talent management to drive into the daily (tactical) work, the roles of all stakeholders must be clarified and accountabilities for those roles must be established.

CEOs have the most important roles to play in their organizations. They champion the need for talent management—and hold everyone accountable for it. They may do this by rewarding achievement of measurable talent objectives, punishing nonachievement, or singling out for attention those who do or don't do a good job in developing talent.

NOTES

1. Bill Geist, *The Big 5-Oh* (1997).
2. See   http://www.mckinseyquarterly.com/Organization/Talent/The_war_for_talent_305_abstract)

3. See http://www.workforcealliance.org/site/pp.aspx?c=ci JNK1PJJtH&b=1151771

4. See http://journals.democraticunderground.com/Lone_ Star_Dem/28.

5. See http://www.whitehouse.gov/cea/cea_immigration_ 062007.html.

6. W. Rothwell (2005) *Effective Succession Planning* (3rd ed) (New York: AMACOM).

Appendix II

A Daily Calendar for the Manager in Talent Management

Directions: What appears below is the start of a daily calendar for 365 days' worth of activities to attract, develop, and maintain talent. It is geared to what you could do every day to attract, develop, and retain talent. Pull out a day/date calendar and adapt this list to your unit, department, division, or organization. There is nothing particularly sacred about this list. But also remember that you can also do things over weekends—like send out e-mails or letters—so that you can do something *every day.* Use your day/date calendar to plan *specific things to do on a daily basis* to manage and develop individuals who are talented people. Identify specific employees in your area of responsibility with whom you can do these things. There is no problem in repeating these activities. Many items below are repeated, and you can no doubt think of additional ways to manage/develop talent on a daily basis with individuals or groups.

Day 1	Have a short meeting with your workers to stress the importance of developing themselves and the importance of them taking an active role in their own development
Day 2	Identify important positions and people in your department and consider how long it would take to replace each one of them in the event of emergency. Plan to source and develop talent to at least cut the time it would take to find and train a replacement for each key person and key position.
Day 3	Develop a profile/description of an ideal performer for each key position and then compare existing staff to that profile/description. What gaps exist? How can people be developed to fill key positions?
Day 4	Consider the organization's strategic objectives and how they impact your organization. Then develop a profile of ideal performers in the future to align with the strategic objectives.
Day 5	Identify the most promotable 10 percent of people in your area of responsibility and consider how to systematically prepare them for promotion
Day 6	Develop a list of short-term back ups to fill in for people who are sick or on vacation
Day 7	Research where you recruited your best people from and plan for getting more from the same sources
Day 8	Examine how selection methods are handled in your area of responsibility and brainstorm a list of ways to improve them. Involve your best people in this process.
Day 9	Develop a systematic approach to developing staff members so that they are promotable
Day 10	Meet with one of your best performers and discuss his or her career plans
Day 11	Take aside one person from your group and offer career advice
Day 12	Walk among your workers and offer encouragement in what they are doing
Day 13	Praise one worker in public for what he or she has done
Day 14	Take one worker aside and privately offer constructive criticism about how he or she could improve work

Day 15	Make it a goal to offer feedback to every individual who reports to you today
Day 16	Offer encouragement to one of your high-potential workers today
Day 17	Identify a high professional (in-house expert) in your area of responsibility and suggest that he or she mentor others
Day 18	Take steps to encourage people with valuable personal contacts to mentor others
Day 19	Take one of your best workers aside and ask what he or she finds most rewarding and least rewarding about the work setting. Then resolve to take steps to enhance what is most rewarding and try to knock down barriers that keep the work setting from being rewarding.
Day 20	Identify people who are diverse and find ways to celebrate, in front of others, what makes them unique
Day 21	Pinpoint someone who is not performing their work or not getting along effectively with others and sit that person down to give him or her specific advice about what he or she could do to improve
Day 22	Reflect on how well you model enthusiasm for self-development and find one way today to show others how you are trying to improve yourself or stay current professionally
Day 23	Pick one of your best people and offer individual coaching in private about what he or she could do to develop himself or herself
Day 24	Prepare individual development plans for your high potentials and meet with them individually to discuss how they could develop themselves for higher level responsibility
Day 25	Find a way to recognize publicly an individual who is doing a good job in developing himself or herself
Day 26	Examine how well your department is developing short-term and long-term back ups
Day 27	Meet with individuals who are being developed as short-term and long-term back ups, giving them feedback and encouragement on their development

Day 28	Single out one of your workers and compliment him or her on what he or she is doing
Day 29	Send an email to one of your workers to offer appreciation for what he or she has done for the work unit and suggest ways that he or she could develop further
Day 30	Meet with one of your best performers and discuss his or her career plans
Day 31	Take aside one person from your group and offer career advice
Day 32	Walk among your workers and offer encouragement in what they are doing
Day 33	Praise one worker in public for what he or she has done
Day 34	Take one worker aside and privately offer constructive criticism about how he or she could improve work
Day 35	Make it a goal to offer individualized feedback to every individual who reports to you today
Day 36	Offer encouragement to one of your high-potential workers today
Day 37	Identify a high professional (in-house expert) in your area of responsibility and suggest that he or she mentor others
Day 38	Take steps to encourage people with valuable personal contacts to mentor others
Day 39	Identify people who are diverse and find ways to celebrate, in front of others, what makes them unique
Day 40	Pinpoint someone who is not performing their work or not getting along effectively with others and sit that person down to give him or her specific advice about what he or she could do to improve
Day 41	Reflect on how well you model enthusiasm for self-development and find one way today to show others how you are trying to improve yourself or stay current professionally
Day 42	Pick one of your best people and offer individual coaching in private about what he or she could do to develop himself or herself
Day 43	Prepare individual development plans for your high potentials and meet with them individually to discuss how they could develop themselves for higher level responsibility

Day 44	Find a way to recognize publicly an individual who is doing a good job in developing himself or herself
Day 45	Examine how well your department is developing short-term and long-term back ups
Day 46	Meet with individuals who are being developed as short-term and long-term back ups, giving them feedback and encouragement on their development
Day 47	Single out one of your workers and compliment him or her on what he or she is doing
Day 48	Send an email to one of your workers to offer appreciation for what he or she has done for the work unit and suggest ways that he or she could develop further
Day 49	Meet with one of your best performers and discuss his or her career plans
Day 50	Take aside one person from your group and offer career advice
Day 51	Walk among your workers and offer encouragement in what they are doing
Day 52	Praise one worker in public for what he or she has done
Day 53	Take one worker aside and privately offer constructive criticism about how he or she could improve work
Day 54	Make it a goal to offer feedback to every individual who reports to you today
Day 55	Offer encouragement to one of your high-potential workers today
Day 56	Identify a high professional (in-house expert) in your area of responsibility and suggest that he or she mentor others
Day 57	Take steps to encourage people with valuable personal contacts to mentor others
Day 58	Identify people who are diverse and find ways to celebrate, in front of others, what makes them unique
Day 59	Reflect on how well you model enthusiasm for self-development and find one way today to show others how you are trying to improve yourself or stay current professionally

Day 60	Single out one worker for special praise and hold a meeting so that all members of the group take turns talking about the strengths of this worker and how he or she could leverage them to advantage
Day 61	Hold a pizza party with your workers to show appreciation for their hard work—and encourage them as a group to discuss ways they could develop themselves further
Day 62	Identify a high professional (in-house expert) in your area of responsibility and suggest that he or she mentor others
Day 63	Take steps to encourage people with valuable personal contacts to mentor others
Day 64	Take one of your best workers aside and ask what he or she finds most rewarding and least rewarding about the work setting. Then resolve to take steps to enhance what is most rewarding and try to knock down barriers that keep the work setting from being rewarding.
Day 65	Identify people who are diverse and find ways to celebrate, in front of others, what makes them unique
Day 66	Pinpoint someone who is not performing their work or not getting along effectively with others and sit that person down to give him or her specific advice about what he or she could do to improve
Day 67	Reflect on how well you model enthusiasm for self-development and find one way today to show others how you are trying to improve yourself or stay current professionally
Day 68	Pick one of your best people and offer individual coaching in private about what he or she could do to develop himself or herself
Day 69	Prepare individual development plans for your high potentials and meet with them individually to discuss how they could develop themselves for higher level responsibility
Day 70	Find a way to recognize publicly an individual who is doing a good job in developing himself or herself
Day 71	Examine how well your department is developing short-term and long-term back ups
Day 72	Meet with individuals who are being developed as short-term and long-term back ups, giving them feedback and encouragement on their development

Day 73	Single out one of your workers and compliment him or her on what he or she is doing
Day 74	Send an email to one of your workers to offer appreciation for what he or she has done for the work unit and suggest ways that he or she could develop further
Day 75	Meet with one of your best performers and discuss his or her career plans
Day 76	Take aside one person from your group and offer career advice
Day 77	Walk among your workers and offer encouragement in what they are doing
Day 78	Praise one worker in public for what he or she has done
Day 79	Take one worker aside and privately offer constructive criticism about how he or she could improve work
Day 80	Make it a goal to offer individualized feedback to every individual who reports to you today
Day 81	Offer encouragement to one of your high-potential workers today
Day 82	Identify a high professional (in-house expert) in your area of responsibility and suggest that he or she mentor others
Day 83	Take steps to encourage people with valuable personal contacts to mentor others
Day 84	Identify people who are diverse and find ways to celebrate, in front of others, what makes them unique
Day 85	Identify a high professional (in-house expert) in your area of responsibility and suggest that he or she mentor others
Day 86	Take steps to encourage people with valuable personal contacts to mentor others
Day 87	Take one of your best workers aside and ask what he or she finds most rewarding and least rewarding about the work setting. Then resolve to take steps to enhance what is most rewarding and try to knock down barriers that keep the work setting from being rewarding.
Day 88	Identify people who are diverse and find ways to celebrate, in front of others, what makes them unique

Day 89	Pinpoint someone who is not performing their work or not getting along effectively with others and sit that person down to give him or her specific advice about what he or she could do to improve
Day 90	Reflect on how well you model enthusiasm for self-development and find one way today to show others how you are trying to improve yourself or stay current professionally
Day 91	Pick one of your best people and offer individual coaching in private about what he or she could do to develop himself or herself
Day 92	Prepare individual development plans for your high potentials and meet with them individually to discuss how they could develop themselves for higher level responsibility
Day 93	Find a way to recognize publicly an individual who is doing a good job in developing himself or herself
Day 94	Examine how well your department is developing short-term and long-term back ups
Day 95	Meet with individuals who are being developed as short-term and long-term back ups, giving them feedback and encouragement on their development
Day 96	Single out one of your workers and compliment him or her on what he or she is doing
Day 97	Send an email to one of your workers to offer appreciation for what he or she has done for the work unit and suggest ways that he or she could develop further
Day 98	Meet with one of your best performers and discuss his or her career plans
Day 99	Take aside one person from your group and offer career advice
Day 100	Praise one worker in public for what he or she has done
Day 101	Take one worker aside and privately offer constructive criticism about how he or she could improve work
Day 102	Make it a goal to offer individualized feedback to every individual who reports to you today
Day 103	Offer encouragement to one of your high-potential workers today
Day 104	Identify a high professional (in-house expert) in your area of responsibility and suggest that he or she mentor others

Day 105	Take steps to encourage people with valuable personal contacts to mentor others
Day 106	Meet with one of your best performers and discuss his or her career plans
Day 107	Take aside one person from your group and offer career advice
Day 108	Walk among your workers and offer encouragement in what they are doing
Day 109	Praise one worker in public for what he or she has done
Day 110	Take one worker aside and privately offer constructive criticism about how he or she could improve work
Day 111	Make it a goal to offer feedback to every individual who reports to you today
Day 112	Offer encouragement to one of your high-potential workers today
Day 113	Take steps to encourage people with valuable personal contacts to mentor others
Day 114	Take one of your best workers aside and ask what he or she finds most rewarding and least rewarding about the work setting. Then resolve to take steps to enhance what is most rewarding and try to knock down barriers that keep the work setting from being rewarding.
Day 115	Identify people who are diverse and find ways to celebrate, in front of others, what makes them unique
Day 116	Pinpoint someone who is not performing their work or not getting along effectively with others and sit that person down to give him or her specific advice about what he or she could do to improve
Day 117	Reflect on how well you model enthusiasm for self-development and find one way today to show others how you are trying to improve yourself or stay current professionally
Day 118	Pick one of your best people and offer individual coaching in private about what he or she could do to develop himself or herself
Day 119	Prepare individual development plans for your high potentials and meet with them individually to discuss how they could develop themselves for higher level responsibility

Day 120	Have a short meeting with your workers to stress the importance of developing themselves and the importance of them taking an active role in their own development
Day 121	Identify important positions and people in your department and consider how long it would take to replace each one of them in the event of emergency. Plan to source and develop talent to at least cut the time it would take to find and train a replacement for each key person and key position.
Day 122	Develop a profile/description of an ideal performer for each key position and then compare existing staff to that profile/description. What gaps exist? How can people be developed to fill key positions?
Day 123	Consider the organization's strategic objectives and how they impact your organization. Then develop a profile of ideal performers in the future to align with the strategic objectives.
Day 124	Identify the most promotable 10 percent of people in your area of responsibility and consider how to systematically prepare them for promotion
Day 125	Develop a list of short-term back ups to fill in for people who are sick or are on vacation
Day 126	Research where you recruited your best people from and plan for getting more from the same sources
Day 127	Examine how selection methods are handled in your area of responsibility and brainstorm a list of ways to improve them. Involve your best people in this process.
Day 128	Develop a systematic approach to developing staff members so that they are promotable
Day 129	Meet with one of your best performers and discuss his or her career plans
Day 130	Take aside one person from your group and offer career advice
Day 131	Walk among your workers and offer encouragement in what they are doing
Day 132	Praise one worker in public for what he or she has done
Day 133	Take one worker aside and privately offer constructive criticism about how he or she could improve work

Day 134	Make it a goal to offer feedback to every individual who reports to you today
Day 135	Offer encouragement to one of your high-potential workers today
Day 136	Identify a high professional (in-house expert) in your area of responsibility and suggest that he or she mentor others
Day 137	Take steps to encourage people with valuable personal contacts to mentor others
Day 138	Take one of your best workers aside and ask what he or she finds most rewarding and least rewarding about the work setting. Then resolve to take steps to enhance what is most rewarding and try to knock down barriers that keep the work setting from being rewarding.
Day 139	Identify people who are diverse and find ways to celebrate, in front of others, what makes them unique
Day 140	Pinpoint someone who is not performing their work or not getting along effectively with others and sit that person down to give him or her specific advice about what he or she could do to improve
Day 141	Reflect on how well you model enthusiasm for self-development and find one way today to show others how you are trying to improve yourself or stay current professionally
Day 142	Pick one of your best people and offer individual coaching in private about what he or she could do to develop himself or herself
Day 143	Prepare individual development plans for your high potentials and meet with them individually to discuss how they could develop themselves for higher level responsibility
Day 144	Find a way to recognize publicly an individual who is doing a good job in developing himself or herself
Day 145	Examine how well your department is developing short-term and long-term back ups
Day 146	Meet with individuals who are being developed as short-term and long-term back ups, giving them feedback and encouragement on their development
Day 147	Single out one of your workers and compliment him or her on what he or she is doing

Day 148	Send an email to one of your workers to offer appreciation for what he or she has done for the work unit and suggest ways that he or she could develop further
Day 149	Meet with one of your best performers and discuss his or her career plans
Day 150	Take aside one person from your group and offer career advice
Day 151	Walk among your workers and offer encouragement in what they are doing
Day 152	Praise one worker in public for what he or she has done
Day 153	Take one worker aside and privately offer constructive criticism about how he or she could improve work
Day 154	Make it a goal to offer individualized feedback to every individual who reports to you today
Day 155	Offer encouragement to one of your high-potential workers today
Day 156	Identify a high professional (in-house expert) in your area of responsibility and suggest that he or she mentor others
Day 157	Take steps to encourage people with valuable personal contacts to mentor others
Day 158	Identify people who are diverse and find ways to celebrate, in front of others, what makes them unique
Day 159	Pinpoint someone who is not performing their work or not getting along effectively with others and sit that person down to give him or her specific advice about what he or she could do to improve
Day 160	Reflect on how well you model enthusiasm for self-development and find one way today to show others how you are trying to improve yourself or stay current professionally
Day 161	Pick one of your best people and offer individual coaching in private about what he or she could do to develop himself or herself
Day 162	Prepare individual development plans for your high potentials and meet with them individually to discuss how they could develop themselves for higher level responsibility
Day 163	Find a way to recognize publicly an individual who is doing a good job in developing himself or herself

Day 164	Examine how well your department is developing short-term and long-term back ups
Day 165	Meet with individuals who are being developed as short-term and long-term back ups, giving them feedback and encouragement on their development
Day 166	Single out one of your workers and compliment him or her on what he or she is doing
Day 167	Send an email to one of your workers to offer appreciation for what he or she has done for the work unit and suggest ways that he or she could develop further
Day 168	Meet with one of your best performers and discuss his or her career plans
Day 169	Take aside one person from your group and offer career advice
Day 170	Walk among your workers and offer encouragement in what they are doing
Day 171	Praise one worker in public for what he or she has done
Day 172	Take one worker aside and privately offer constructive criticism about how he or she could improve work
Day 173	Make it a goal to offer individualized feedback to every individual who reports to you today
Day 174	Offer encouragement to one of your high-potential workers today
Day 175	Identify a high professional (in-house expert) in your area of responsibility and suggest that he or she mentor others
Day 176	Take steps to encourage people with valuable personal contacts to mentor others
Day 177	Identify people who are diverse and find ways to celebrate, in front of others, what makes them unique
Day 178	Single out one worker for special praise and hold a meeting so that all members of the group take turns talking about the strengths of this worker and how he or she could leverage them to advantage
Day 179	Hold a pizza party with your workers to show appreciation for their hard work—and encourage them as a group to discuss ways they could develop themselves further

Day 180	Purchase a copy of *1001 Ways to Reward Employees* and adapt it to talent management
Day 181	Use an adapted activity from *1001 Ways to Reward Employees* with one employee or a group
Day 182	Have a short meeting with your workers to stress the importance of developing themselves and the importance of them taking an active role in their own development
Day 183	Identify important positions and people in your department and consider how long it would take to replace each one of them in the event of emergency. Plan to source and develop talent to at least cut the time it would take to find and train a replacement for each key person and key position.
Day 184	Develop a profile/description of an ideal performer for each key position and then compare existing staff to that profile/description. What gaps exist? How can people be developed to fill key positions?
Day 185	Consider the organization's strategic objectives and how they impact your organization. Then develop a profile of ideal performers in the future to align with the strategic objectives.
Day 186	Identify the most promotable 10 percent of people in your area of responsibility and consider how to systematically prepare them for promotion
Day 187	Develop a list of short-term back ups to fill in for people who are sick or are on vacation
Day 188	Research where you recruited your best people from and plan for getting more from the same sources
Day 189	Examine how selection methods are handled in your area of responsibility and brainstorm a list of ways to improve them. Involve your best people in this process.
Day 190	Develop a systematic approach to developing staff members so that they are promotable
Day 191	Meet with one of your best performers and discuss his or her career plans
Day 192	Take aside one person from your group and offer career advice
Day 193	Walk among your workers and offer encouragement in what they are doing

Day 194	Praise one worker in public for what he or she has done
Day 195	Take one worker aside and privately offer constructive criticism about how he or she could improve work
Day 196	Make it goal to offer feedback to every individual who reports to you today
Day 197	Offer encouragement to one of your high-potential workers today
Day 198	Identify a high professional (in-house expert) in your area of responsibility and suggest that he or she mentor others
Day 199	Take steps to encourage people with valuable personal contacts to mentor others
Day 200	Take one of your best workers aside and ask what he or she finds most rewarding and least rewarding about the work setting. Then resolve to take steps to enhance what is most rewarding and try to knock down barriers that keep the work setting from being rewarding.
Day 201	Identify people who are diverse and find ways to celebrate, in front of others, what makes them unique
Day 202	Pinpoint someone who is not performing their work or not getting along effectively with others and sit that person down to give him or her specific advice about what he or she could do to improve
Day 203	Reflect on how well you model enthusiasm for self-development and find one way today to show others how you are trying to improve yourself or stay current professionally
Day 204	Pick one of your best people and offer individual coaching in private about what he or she could do to develop himself or herself
Day 205	Prepare individual development plans for your high potentials and meet with them individually to discuss how they could develop themselves for higher level responsibility
Day 206	Find a way to recognize publicly an individual who is doing a good job in developing himself or herself
Day 207	Examine how well your department is developing short-term and long-term back ups
Day 208	Meet with individuals who are being developed as short-term and long-term back ups, giving them feedback and encouragement on their development
Day 209	Single out one of your workers and compliment him or her on what he or she is doing

Day 210	Send an email to one of your workers to offer appreciation for what he or she has done for the work unit and suggest ways that he or she could develop further
Day 211	Meet with one of your best performers and discuss his or her career plans
Day 212	Take aside one person from your group and offer career advice
Day 213	Walk among your workers and offer encouragement in what they are doing
Day 214	Praise one worker in public for what he or she has done
Day 215	Take one worker aside and privately offer constructive criticism about how he or she could improve work
Day 216	Make it a goal to offer individualized feedback to every individual who reports to you today
Day 217	Offer encouragement to one of your high-potential workers today
Day 218	Identify a high professional (in-house expert) in your area of responsibility and suggest that he or she mentor others
Day 219	Take steps to encourage people with valuable personal contacts to mentor others
Day 220	Identify people who are diverse and find ways to celebrate, in front of others, what makes them unique
Day 221	Demonstrate how to coach to workers and encourage them to coach each other
Day 222	Purchase a copy of *1001 Ways to Recognize Employees* and adapt it to talent management
Day 223	Use an adapted activity from *1001 Ways to Reward Employees* with one employee or a group
Day 224	Have a short meeting with your workers to stress the importance of developing themselves and the importance of them taking an active role in their own development
Day 225	Identify important positions and people in your department and consider how long it would take to replace each one of them in the event of emergency. Plan to source and develop talent to at least cut the time it would take to find and train a replacement for each key person and key position.

Day 226	Develop a profile/description of an ideal performer for each key position and then compare existing staff to that profile/description. What gaps exist? How can people be developed to fill key positions?
Day 227	Consider the organization's strategic objectives and how they impact your organization. Then develop a profile of ideal performers in the future to align with the strategic objectives.
Day 228	Take one of your best workers aside and ask what he or she finds most rewarding and least rewarding about the work setting. Then resolve to take steps to enhance what is most rewarding and try to knock down barriers that keep the work setting from being rewarding.
Day 229	Identify people who are diverse and find ways to celebrate, in front of others, what makes them unique
Day 230	Pinpoint someone who is not performing their work or not getting along effectively with others and sit that person down to give him or her specific advice about what he or she could do to improve
Day 231	Reflect on how well you model enthusiasm for self-development and find one way today to show others how you are trying to improve yourself or stay current professionally
Day 232	Pick one of your best people and offer individual coaching in private about what he or she could do to develop himself or herself
Day 233	Prepare individual development plans for your high potentials and meet with them individually to discuss how they could develop themselves for higher level responsibility
Day 234	Find a way to recognize publicly an individual who is doing a good job in developing himself or herself
Day 235	Examine how well your department is developing short-term and long-term back ups
Day 236	Meet with individuals who are being developed as short-term and long-term back ups, giving them feedback and encouragement on their development
Day 237	Single out one of your workers and compliment him or her on what he or she is doing

Day 238	Send an email to one of your workers to offer appreciation for what he or she has done for the work unit and suggest ways that he or she could develop further
Day 239	Meet with one of your best performers and discuss his or her career plans
Day 240	Take aside one person from your group and offer career advice
Day 241	Walk among your workers and offer encouragement in what they are doing
Day 242	Praise one worker in public for what he or she has done
Day 243	Take one worker aside and privately offer constructive criticism about how he or she could improve work
Day 244	Make it a goal to offer individualized feedback to every individual who reports to you today
Day 245	Offer encouragement to one of your high-potential workers today
Day 246	Identify a high professional (in-house expert) in your area of responsibility and suggest that he or she mentor others
Day 247	Take steps to encourage people with valuable personal contacts to mentor others
Day 248	Identify people who are diverse and find ways to celebrate, in front of others, what makes them unique
Day 249	Research where you recruited your best people from and plan for getting more from the same sources
Day 250	Examine how selection methods are handled in your area of responsibility and brainstorm a list of ways to improve them. Involve your best people in this process.
Day 251	Develop a systematic approach to developing staff members so that they are promotable
Day 252	Meet with one of your best performers and discuss his or her career plans
Day 253	Take aside one person from your group and offer career advice
Day 254	Walk among your workers and offer encouragement in what they are doing
Day 255	Praise one worker in public for what he or she has done

Day 256	Take one worker aside and privately offer constructive criticism about how he or she could improve work
Day 257	Make it a goal to offer feedback to every individual who reports to you today
Day 258	Offer encouragement to one of your high-potential workers today
Day 259	Identify a high professional (in-house expert) in your area of responsibility and suggest that he or she mentor others
Day 260	Take steps to encourage people with valuable personal contacts to mentor others
Day 261	Take one of your best workers aside and ask what he or she finds most rewarding and least rewarding about the work setting. Then resolve to take steps to enhance what is most rewarding and try to knock down barriers that keep the work setting from being rewarding.
Day 262	Identify people who are diverse and find ways to celebrate, in front of others, what makes them unique
Day 263	Pinpoint someone who is not performing their work or not getting along effectively with others and sit that person down to give him or her specific advice about what he or she could do to improve
Day 264	Reflect on how well you model enthusiasm for self-development and find one way today to show others how you are trying to improve yourself or stay current professionally
Day 265	Pick one of your best people and offer individual coaching in private about what he or she could do to develop himself or herself
Day 266	Prepare individual development plans for your high potentials and meet with them individually to discuss how they could develop themselves for higher level responsibility
Day 267	Find a way to recognize publicly an individual who is doing a good job in developing himself or herself
Day 268	Examine how well your department is developing short-term and long-term back ups
Day 269	Meet with individuals who are being developed as short-term and long-term back ups, giving them feedback and encouragement on their development
Day 270	Single out one of your workers and compliment him or her on what he or she is doing

Day 271	Send an email to one of your workers to offer appreciation for what he or she has done for the work unit and suggest ways that he or she could develop further
Day 272	Meet with one of your best performers and discuss his or her career plans
Day 273	Take aside one person from your group and offer career advice
Day 274	Walk among your workers and offer encouragement in what they are doing
Day 275	Praise one worker in public for what he or she has done
Day 276	Take one worker aside and privately offer constructive criticism about how he or she could improve work
Day 277	Make it a goal to offer individualized feedback to every individual who reports to you today
Day 278	Offer encouragement to one of your high-potential workers today
Day 279	Identify a high professional (in-house expert) in your area of responsibility and suggest that he or she mentor others
Day 280	Take steps to encourage people with valuable personal contacts to mentor others
Day 281	Identify people who are diverse and find ways to celebrate, in front of others, what makes them unique
Day 282	Demonstrate how to coach to workers and encourage them to coach each other
Day 283	Use an adapted activity from *1001 Ways to Recognize Employees* with one employee or a group
Day 284	Brainstorm approaches to build talent with your employees every day with other managers in your organization and apply one of those methods with one employee or a group in your department or in other departments
Day 285	Have a short meeting with your workers to stress the importance of developing themselves and the importance of them taking an active role in their own development
Day 286	Identify important positions and people in your department and consider how long it would take to replace each one of them in the event of emergency. Plan to source and develop talent to at least cut the time it would take to find and train a replacement for each key person and key position.

Day 287	Develop a profile/description of an ideal performer for each key position and then compare existing staff to that profile/description. What gaps exist? How can people be developed to fill key positions?
Day 288	Share the profile/description of an ideal performer for each key position with some of your high potentials and ask for their thoughts on how they could develop themselves to match the profile.
Day 289	Pick a high potential worker and ask him or her whether he or she wants to be promoted.
Day 290	Take one of your best workers aside and ask what he or she finds most rewarding and least rewarding about the work setting. Then resolve to take steps to enhance what is most rewarding and try to knock down barriers that keep the work setting from being rewarding.
Day 291	Identify people who are diverse and find ways to celebrate, in front of others, what makes them unique
Day 292	Pinpoint someone who is not performing their work or not getting along effectively with others and sit that person down to give him or her specific advice about what he or she could do to improve
Day 293	Reflect on how well you model enthusiasm for self-development and find one way today to show others how you are trying to improve yourself or stay current professionally
Day 294	Pick one of your best people and offer individual coaching in private about what he or she could do to develop himself or herself
Day 295	Prepare individual development plans for your high potentials and meet with them individually to discuss how they could develop themselves for higher level responsibility
Day 296	Find a way to recognize publicly an individual who is doing a good job in developing himself or herself
Day 297	Examine how well your department is developing short-term and long-term back ups
Day 298	Meet with individuals who are being developed as short-term and long-term back ups, giving them feedback and encouragement on their development
Day 299	Single out one of your workers and compliment him or her on what he or she is doing

Day 300	Send an email to one of your workers to offer appreciation for what he or she has done for the work unit and suggest ways that he or she could develop further
Day 301	Meet with one of your best performers and discuss his or her career plans
Day 302	Take aside one person from your group and offer career advice
Day 303	Walk among your workers and offer encouragement in what they are doing
Day 304	Praise one worker in public for what he or she has done
Day 305	Take one worker aside and privately offer constructive criticism about how he or she could improve work
Day 306	Make it a target to offer individualized feedback to every individual who reports to you today
Day 307	Offer encouragement to one of your high-potential workers today
Day 308	Identify a high professional (in-house expert) in your area of responsibility and suggest that he or she mentor others
Day 309	Take steps to encourage people with valuable personal contacts to mentor others
Day 310	Identify people who are diverse and find ways to celebrate, in front of others, what makes them unique
Day 311	Demonstrate how to coach to workers and encourage them to coach each other
Day 312	Use an adapted activity from *1001 Ways to Reward Employees* with one employee or a group
Day 313	Use an approach that you brainstormed with other managers in your organization to build talent with your employees and apply one of those methods with one employee or a group in your department or in other departments
Day 314	Have a short meeting with your workers to stress the importance of developing themselves and the importance of them taking an active role in their own development
Day 315	Identify important positions and people in your department and consider how long it would take to replace each one of them in the event of emergency. Plan to source and develop talent to at least cut the time it would take to find and train a replacement for each key person and key position.

Day 316	Develop a profile/description of an ideal performer for each key position and then compare existing staff to that profile/description. What gaps exist? How can people be developed to fill key positions?
Day 317	Consider the organization's strategic objectives and how they impact your organization. Then develop a profile of ideal performers in the future to align with the strategic objectives.
Day 318	Identify the most promotable 10 percent of people in your area of responsibility and consider how to systematically prepare them for promotion
Day 319	Develop a list of short-term back ups to fill in for people who are sick or are on vacation
Day 320	Research where you recruited your best people from and plan for getting more from the same sources
Day 321	Examine how selection methods are handled in your area of responsibility and brainstorm a list of ways to improve them. Involve your best people in this process.
Day 322	Develop a systematic approach to developing staff members so that they are promotable
Day 323	Meet with one of your best performers and discuss his or her career plans
Day 324	Take aside one person from your group and offer career advice
Day 325	Walk among your workers and offer encouragement in what they are doing
Day 326	Praise one worker in public for what he or she has done
Day 327	Take one worker aside and privately offer constructive criticism about how he or she could improve work
Day 328	Make it a goal to offer feedback to every individual who reports to you today
Day 329	Offer encouragement to one of your high-potential workers today
Day 330	Identify a high professional (in-house expert) in your area of responsibility and suggest that he or she mentor others
Day 331	Make it a goal to offer individualized feedback to every individual who reports to you today

Day 332	Offer encouragement to one of your high-potential workers today
Day 333	Identify a high professional (in-house expert) in your area of responsibility and suggest that he or she mentor others
Day 334	Take steps to encourage people with valuable personal contacts to mentor others
Day 335	Take one of your best workers aside and ask what he or she finds most rewarding and least rewarding about the work setting. Then resolve to take steps to enhance what is most rewarding and try to knock down barriers that keep the work setting from being rewarding.
Day 336	Identify people who are diverse and find ways to celebrate, in front of others, what makes them unique
Day 337	Pinpoint someone who is not performing their work or not getting along effectively with others and sit that person down to give him or her specific advice about what he or she could do to improve
Day 338	Reflect on how well you model enthusiasm for self-development and find one way today to show others how you are trying to improve yourself or stay current professionally
Day 339	Pick one of your best people and offer individual coaching in private about what he or she could do to develop himself or herself
Day 340	Prepare individual development plans for your high potentials and meet with them individually to discuss how they could develop themselves for higher-level responsibility
Day 341	Find a way to recognize publicly an individual who is doing a good job in developing himself or herself
Day 342	Examine how well your department is developing short-term and long-term back ups
Day 343	Meet with individuals who are being developed as short-term and long-term back ups, giving them feedback and encouragement on their development
Day 344	Single out one of your workers and compliment him or her on what he or she is doing
Day 345	Send an email to one of your workers to offer appreciation for what he or she has done for the work unit and suggest ways that he or she could develop further

Day 346	Meet with one of your best performers and discuss his or her career plans
Day 347	Take aside one person from your group and offer career advice
Day 348	Walk among your workers and offer encouragement in what they are doing
Day 349	Praise one worker in public for what he or she has done
Day 350	Take one worker aside and privately offer constructive criticism about how he or she could improve work
Day 351	Make it a goal to offer individualized feedback to every individual who reports to you today
Day 352	Offer encouragement to one of your high-potential workers today
Day 353	Identify a high professional (in-house expert) in your area of responsibility and suggest that he or she mentor others
Day 354	Pinpoint someone who is not performing their work, or not getting along effectively with others, and sit that person down to give him or her specific advice about what he or she could do to improve
Day 355	Reflect on how well you model enthusiasm for self-development and find one way today to show others how you are trying to improve yourself or stay current professionally
Day 356	Pick one of your best people and offer individual coaching in private about what he or she could do to develop himself or herself
Day 357	Prepare individual development plans for your high potentials and meet with them individually to discuss how they could develop themselves for higher level responsibility
Day 358	Find a way to recognize publicly an individual who is doing a good job in developing himself or herself
Day 359	Examine how well your department is developing short-term and long-term back ups
Day 360	Meet with individuals who are being developed as short-term and long-term back ups, giving them feedback and encouragement on their development
Day 361	Single out one of your workers and compliment him or her on what he or she is doing

Day 362	Send an email to one of your workers to offer appreciation for what he or she has done for the work unit and suggest ways that he or she could develop further
Day 363	Meet with one of your best performers and discuss his or her career plans
Day 364	Take aside one person from your group and offer career advice
Day 365	Walk among your workers and offer encouragement in what they are doing

Note: Think about forming a group of managers inside your organization and asking them to brainstorm their own company-specific list of daily actions that can be taken to develop talent. That is a good way to bring visibility to the effort and reinforce the point that it should be a daily responsibility of managers. And remember: you don't have to be at work to do some of these things. Emails and voice mails can be sent out on weekends, for instance.

Index

Index

About the Author

William J. Rothwell, Ph.D., SPHR, is President of Rothwell and Associates, Inc. (see www.rothwell-associates.com), a full-service consulting firm that offers services in Succession Planning and Management. He is also a Professor in the Workforce Education and Development program in the Department of Learning and Performance Systems on the University Park campus of The Pennsylvania State University.

Before arriving at Penn State, he was Assistant Vice President and Management Development Director for The Franklin Life Insurance Co., a wholly owned subsidiary of a Fortune 48 corporation at the time of his employment. Before that, he was Training Director for the Illinois Office of the Auditor General.

Dr. Rothwell was National Thought Leader for a Linkage-DDI sponsored study of 18 multinational corporations in 2001 that examined corporate best practices in succession planning and management. His bestselling book *Effective Succession Planning: Ensuring Leadership Continuity and Building Talent from Within,* 3rd ed. (New York: Amacom, 2005) is regarded by some as the "corporate bible" on succession management practices. His books include *Career Planning and Succession Management* (Westport, CT: Greenwood/Praeger, 2005), *Next Generation Management Development* (San Francisco: Pfeiffer, 2007), *HR Transformation: Demonstrating Strategic Leadership in the Face of Future Trends* (Davies-Black, 2008), *Working Longer: New Strategies for Managing, Training, and Retaining Older*

253

Employees (New York: Amacom, 2008), *Adult Learning Basics* (Alexandria, VA: ASTD Press, 2008), *Cases in Government Succession Planning: Action-Oriented Strategies for Public-Sector Human Capital Management, Workforce Planning, Succession Planning, and Talent Management* (Amherst, MA: HRD Press, 2008), and *Cases in Linking Workforce Development to Economic Development: Community College Partnering For Training, Individual Career Planning, And Community And Economic Development* (Washington: American Association of Community Colleges, 2008).

He is also author or coauthor of such related books as *Building In-House Leadership and Management Development Programs* (Westport, CT: Quorum Books, 1999), *The Competency Toolkit,* 2 vols. (Amherst, MA: Human Resource Development Press, 2000), and *The Action Learning Guidebook* (San Francisco: Jossey-Bass, 1999). He has authored, coauthored, edited or coedited over 300 books and articles and has consulted on succession planning and talent management in a wide array of organizations in business, government, and nonprofit settings both in the United States and internationally.

He can be reached at wjr9@psu.edu.